Living on Empty

Living on Empty

Mary Jane Hamilton

VICTOR BOOKS

A DIVISION OF SCRIPTURE PRESS PUBLICATIONS INC.
USA CANADA ENGLAND

Scripture quotations are from the
New American Standard Bible,
© the Lockman Foundation 1960, 1962, 1963,
1968, 1971, 1972, 1973, 1975, 1977.
All rights reserved.

Copyediting: Jane Vogel, Barbara Williams
Cover Design: Scott Rattray

Library of Congress Cataloging-in-Publication Data

Hamilton, Mary Jane, 1946–
    Living on empty / Mary Jane Hamilton.
      p.   cm.
    ISBN 1-56476-391-9
    1. Hamilton, Mary Jane, 1946–   . 2. Christian
biography—United States. 3. Bulimia—Patients—Biography.
4. Adult child sexual abuse victims—United States—Biography.
I. Title.
BR1725.H234A3 1994
[B]248.8'6'092—dc20

                                          94-29494
                                             CIP

---

1 2 3 4 5 6 7 8 9 10 Printing/Year 98 97 96 95 94

For John, Jeff, and Jenny
who know me
and
still love me.

CONTENTS

Foreword

Every life is a story; every story is a glimpse of life. We are surrounded by story every day. The man who just bought a new car tells you about how he got a great deal. The woman, standing in a grocery line, passes the time talking about her daughter—"Things are not the same. I remember coming home with more books than I could carry. My daughter has not had a lick of homework in weeks. It's a crying shame."

What happens when we hear a story? For many it triggers memories (buying my first car), clarifies convictions (kids need more homework), and helps conceive the future (I need a new car too).

In *Walking on Water*, Madeline L'Engle quotes Laurens Van Der Post's observation about the Kalahari Bushman: "The extreme expression of his spirit was in his story. He was a wonderful storyteller. The story was his sacred possession. These people know what we do not—that without a story you have not got a nation, or a culture, or a civilization. Without a story of your own to live you haven't got a life of your own" (p. 140). We remember, comprehend, and create our lives through story. We can't exist without story.

In Mary Jane Hamilton's rich narrative journey we are invited to glimpse a life, a story that has the potential to change our life. *Living on Empty* is one woman's story of awakening to what it means to "taste the Lord and know He is good."

Mary Jane struggled for nearly three decades with a secret, deeply shameful addiction to bulimia. She hid her addiction from her husband, family, and friends. Tragically, her story is not unique; it is estimated that over 8 million women struggle with this battle. What is unique in this book is her perspective about what was involved in her struggle. She goes well beyond the scripted cultural notion that addiction is a "disease."

We live in a culture that has found relief from the ownership of destructive compulsions by relishing the role of a "victim." If we have been harmed by sexual abuse, a dysfunctional family, divorce, or other trauma, then we are stuck in our emptiness; in bondage until we are healed by psychotherapy, recovery, or some other intervention. Law cases abound that give credence to the conviction—We are above the law if we have been damaged. This is insane.

But we have been harmed. We do struggle with the wounds of childhood. How do we grapple with our wounds in light of the biblical supposition that we are utterly responsible for our life, even if we have been hurt or misunderstood? The answer to the question is best answered by story, not by mere abstraction or assertion.

Mary Jane was a victim. She was abused; she experienced significant emptiness in her family. Is this her story? Join her in victimization? Not at all. She weaves a far more complex, far more biblical narrative about how food became her god, her idol. She offers a picture of how the heart can be driven by illusions and lies, and still operate as a virtuous—in appearance, mature Christian—yet be self-righteous and hardened to the opulent whispering of God's love.

Living on Empty is not a simplistic, predictable journey. Mary Jane has traveled through terrain that is full of odd twists and turns. But the road leads to the mystery of God's incomprehensible and uncontrollable love. Her story is captivating. She is captivating. I have witnessed part of her remarkable change—I have been blessed by her gentle strength and persistent kindness. But as remarkable as she is, it is what her life offers to our story that causes me to be so delighted by *Living on Empty*.

Tenderly and honestly, she illumines our journey, our wounds, and idolatry. She compels us to see the profound relationship between heartache and hope; repentance and reconciliation; the Cross and the Resurrection.

Mary Jane is a wonderful storyteller. But more important, her story will help us envision the path to deep change— the kind of change that magnifies Jesus Christ and not any system, person, or process. *Living on Empty* will help you put words to a journey that deeply faces harm, but goes beyond wounds to the kind of idolatry that only repentance and dependence on the Lord can heal. Put your shoes on. Get your pack on. You are in for a story that could change your life.

Dan B. Allender, Ph.D.

Preface

This book deals with the issues of eating disorders, intimacy, and exposure. I have been very fortunate that my husband, John, and my children have embraced me in my secret and pain. They have been supportive through my exposure and have stayed with me in the struggle of coming alive as a woman.

This book may stir up anger or anxiety in women who know their husbands will not respond well to their pain and secrets. Does this excuse your hiding? No! The things we hide are what eventually hurt us the most. The inability to trust is serious, especially in marriage. Anything that is secret will block the bonding God designed for a husband and wife. It is my desire that you would seek help through a trusted friend or a counselor to begin talking about your secrets. Your survival and that of your marriage may depend on it.

If you are single, you can work toward intimacy with God

and friends. Again I hope you would seek help in working through your secrets. Your action now could definitely influence the choices you make in your future relationships.

The purpose of this book is not to expose anyone but myself. I was trapped in the eating disorder of bulimia and vomiting for twenty-five years, and I thought there was no escape. Like 8 million other women caught in this addictive behavior, I tried the conventional ways to quit: counseling, behavioral changes, and support groups. Unlike the majority of these 8 million women, I have found the way out!

The road I traveled during my eating disorder was one of secrecy and hiding. For years no one knew about my struggles. Becoming a Christian had no effect on my behavior. I perpetuated the cycle for fifteen years as a visible and spiritually involved Christian woman. It was scary to arrive at the end of my road and to expose my eating disorder to those who were in a position to reject me. What I found were four people eager to enter my pain and embrace me as a wife, mother and woman.

I know women are looking for the way out of this addictive behavior. You will find that way unfolded in the pages of this book. Recovery is possible only when we stop living on empty and fill our emotional bankruptcy with the food that satisfies our hungry soul.

Acknowledgments

Many heartfelt thanks to:

Nancy Dorner, who proved to be a gracious mentor as she met with me time after time to read, critique, and simultaneously laugh and cry over my story. Her wisdom has been invaluable, but, even more, her friendship, encouragement, and acceptance of who I am have been the strength I've needed to follow through with this project.

Sandy Burdick, who came alongside my wounded spirit and saw value, not only in me, but in the mess I had made of my life. She has been a dear friend whose gentle probing caused me to wonder about God in the midst of my struggle. I'll remember Sandy as the one who entered my pain, embraced my womanhood, and loved me well.

Shirley Bumgardner, who used her fine-tuned, red pen to edit my rough copy. She took a risk on this "rookie writer" as I continually dropped chapters on her desk. I have appreciated her insights on this manuscript and her compassion toward me.

Wes Roberts, who saw my potential and was willing to "go to bat" for me. He has ministered to me from afar with his encouragement, and his spirit has provided a resting place as I remember him as a truly gentle man.

Larry Crabb and **Dan Allender,** who disrupted me, awakened the awareness of sin in my life (boy, did that make me mad!), and gently led me back to God. Those videotapes changed my life, and as I ponder their impact, it is with joy, fondness, and with a heart that says, "Yes, God is indeed good."

John, who has endured this whole process, never doubting God's purpose for my life. He has provided a safe place for me through his patience, strength, and love. I have found that I am enjoying this "safe" place more often now as I meet with him there and realize he has truly become my best friend.

God, who has promised, "For I am confident of this very thing, that He who began a good work in you will perfect it until the day of Christ Jesus" (Philippians 1:6).

Chapter One

The Terrible Trap

Recently I've thought a lot about the words my dad spoke to me when I was seventeen years old. Words that were so powerful they impacted my soul for years to come. Words that became implanted into my existence, never to be forgotten. Words that crushed me, never to be retrieved. Words that replayed as tapes in my head to remind me of the fear I had of being less than perfect for my dad.

It had not been a particularly good summer. I was not dating or working, and I was bored. My senior year was ahead of me, but I was apprehensive about what it would be like. I was feeling ugly, lonely, and out of sync, not only in my body, but in my home. None of my clothes seemed to fit right. They were either too loose or too tight. A bathing suit was a disaster! My body was filling out, but in all the wrong places. I felt like a displaced person.

My brothers had arrived home from their summer in Europe and wondered what had happened to their "little" sister. I had stopped growing up and had grown out.

As I sat across the table from my dad one August night, I wasn't a pretty picture. I was wearing cut-off jeans, a white blouse with the tails out, and tennis shoes. I sported glasses, straight hair, and no makeup. I was hungry, I ate, and I hurt. And there I sat, facing the one person I so much wanted to please. In my pain and emotional distress I had stuffed down five chicken legs right in front of him. I didn't think he had noticed, but he did.

Just Dieting

As I look back, I can see how food became my number-one priority. At the time I would not have admitted that food could mean so much and be so important. But now I see very clearly that food, combined with the secrecy of bulimia, controlled the choices I made for twenty-five years.

It did not start out that way. I was "just dieting." Somewhere in those rocky teenage years I stopped growing up and started growing out. It seemed to happen overnight. Suddenly I saw myself as big. My dad brought it to my attention that night after dinner when I had consumed too much food. Five chicken legs! He was actually counting. I felt this was some kind of game; he was keeping score and I was losing. He glared at me across our kitchen table and said, "Mary Jane, if you continue to eat like that you'll be big and fat. There are a lot of big women on my side of the family, and you'll be just like them." I was horrified and felt like a stuffed pig. Five chicken legs! It had not seemed like a lot to me, but it must have been for him to notice.

Determined to change, I set out to do something about my weight. I knew I could do it, because I wanted to please my dad. Later that night I scrutinized my body in front of a full-length mirror. What I saw was a tall, seventeen-year-old girl who looked big and awkward with hunched shoulders, straggly hair, horn-rimmed glasses, flat chest, and a round tummy. I saw nothing that could be called attractive, and my dad was right—I was getting fat. How could this have happened so quickly? My body had gotten out of control! I needed to do something fast.

I had no idea that what started out innocently as "just a diet" would snowball into such gross and damaging behavior and freeze me into a lifestyle that would numb my very soul and rule my existence for years to come.

The "just dieting" worked very well for about nine months. I became a compulsive student of food and nutrition as I studied the caloric and nutritional value of every morsel that entered my mouth. Heaven forbid that any fat would slip past my lips! That would be disastrous. I ate very small amounts of food to make sure I did not overeat. It was crucial to eliminate all high-calorie food, starch, sugar, and carbohydrates. There was no room for error—I had to stick to low-calorie food. Plain and simple!

Whenever my craving for something sweet and creamy would surface, I allowed myself the pleasure of eating powdered coffee creamer by the teaspoonful straight from the jar. It would dissolve slowly in my mouth and tasted so rich and good. But I had to be very careful I didn't go overboard at ten calories per teaspoon. So my allowance was no more than two spoonfuls.

The "dieting" results were great throughout my senior year. I lost twenty-five pounds, was slim, looked wonderful, and received many compliments on the "new" me. Those positives far outweighed the negatives I remembered: constant hunger, fear of losing control and overeating, not eating out because I could not control what was being served, depriving myself of the enjoyment of any food, weighing myself daily (sometimes after each meal), and isolating myself from friends, fun, and food.

I moved from "just dieting" into dangerous dieting the summer before I left for my freshman year at college. One night I had eaten too much. I felt too full, and the scales said I weighed too much. Could anyone tell just by looking at me that I had lost control of what went into my mouth? Surely, someone would notice that the new slim me was starting to bulge. If only I could get rid of the food! If I swallowed hard enough or drank carbonated soda pop, would it come up? Yes, it would, and it did! Thank goodness I was safe—but unfortunately I felt hungry. Thinking I could eat just a little to appease the hunger pangs, I once again stuffed myself. Dumb, dumb, dumb! I'd just vomit this one more time, and I wouldn't do it again.

So the cycle started, accelerated, and remained in high gear for the next twenty-five years!

Silence and Secrecy

At college I became pretty much a loner. I don't think I set out to be, but I was consumed with thinking of ways to sneak food into my dorm room, to be eaten alone and vomited in secret. I remember going to "mixers" at the union longing to be noticed by someone special, to be singled out by someone who wanted to spend time with me. Sadly, I found myself alone at the end of the evening, disappointed and hungry. Why wouldn't a Coke and an order of fries satisfy me? I craved more—much more, and I brought it back to my room to gorge alone.

Mealtime at the dorm was something to look forward to. I never missed one! Not even on Sunday morning when only a handful of people got up for breakfast. I would rather eat than sleep. I was always hungry. If people noticed how much I ate, I simply went farther into isolation and secrecy. If they wondered how I could eat so much and stay so slim, I lied, boasting of a high metabolism, thin genes, and anxiety. Oh, anxiety—I was truthful on one of the three! I was anxious all right! Who wouldn't be if they had to work as hard as I did to keep my secret intact?

I not only stooped to the level of lying for food, I became a thief too! I remember sneaking into a dorm room and taking a box of crackers, only to consume the whole box in a few short minutes. Then I was horrified that I had stolen something—food, no less. I was terrified of being caught—how shameful. Vomiting made me feel better, and I swore never to steal again. I never did steal from a dorm room, but I did from the cafeteria. But was that really stealing? Wasn't that covered under room and board? After all, it was just an extra dessert, donut, or box of cereal here and there. It was so easy to steal, and I didn't get caught! I ate it so fast that no one ever knew. I was good at what I did in silence and secrecy.

It never occurred to me during this time that I chose my lifestyle because of food. Isolation and distance were survival tactics to hide me and my disgusting behavior. It did not occur to me to try to stop. How could I? Was I capable of quitting? What was required of me? What would happen if I did? I had no answers to those questions, so I continued the eating disorder. I was too ashamed to get help. How would I ever explain to anyone what I was doing? Was there a name for this disorder? I didn't know of one. I was stuck. It had become second nature to me and so familiar as well as safe. As long as I could keep the secret and hide I would not have to face others or myself.

Food had a wonderful way of numbing me out. It took care of my loneliness, rejection, fear, anger, and anxiety. It was soothing to forget while I ate myself into oblivion, feeling absolutely nothing as the food went from my fingers into my mouth. I gorged on anything I wanted but nothing in particular. All food worked to give me comfort and courage to face the day and night ahead of me. I felt no guilt about the amounts of money I spent on food because I never bought anything else for myself. No clothes, no make-up, no jewelry! So I justified that nicely and continued to eat. Only when I had to get rid of the food did guilt, anxiety, and fear surface. But the act of vomiting took only a few short minutes, and the guilt was short-lived until the next time.

Planning for the next time—*what* I would eat, *where* I would eat, and *when* I would eat—gave me a feeling of control and excitement. The act of eating was the top of a roller-coaster, as the numbing pleasure of the food took control and I could forget who I was, where I was, and what I was doing. But the ride took a plunge as I once again bent over the toilet to vomit out all I had consumed. Only when asleep did I feel free of food and its deadening effects. I moved into a paralyzing sleep only to awaken to start the roller-coaster ride once again.

The magical age of twenty-one brought a whole new compulsion for me as I started drinking excessively to match my eating—only to vomit both food and alcohol out of my body. Now alcohol came alongside food to fill me, to lift me, to give me a short period of illegitimate pleasure before I vomited and was again empty, degraded, and miserable. I continued drinking late into my twenties.

How John and I met and later married is nothing short of a miracle, considering that we are still married after twenty-five years. I was needy enough to know I wanted a man, lucky enough to find one, and sneaky enough to continue my secret eating and vomiting at the same time. I had thought that possibly marriage would be the magic cure for this dangerous behavior, but I found myself conjuring up new ways of hiding my disorder as I made the adjustments to married life. It was definitely too late to tell John. I should have done it before we were married, but that seemed too risky. Would he still have married me?

John was a good choice for me because he was kind, unassuming, accepting, and enjoyed everything I cooked. He did not make me feel guilty about the amounts I consumed, and he never questioned the disappearance of food or leftovers. I was pretty safe with John. So I continued to stuff myself and to vomit in secret.

I'll never forget the first time I read a magazine article about eating disorders. I was sitting in the waiting room of a doctor's office, and the word *bulimia* jumped out at me. There was actually a name for my eating and vomiting! I could not even pronounce it, but I could sure practice it. I remember my face getting warm and flushed as I perched on the edge of my seat, wanting to hide the article from the lady sitting next to me. I felt exposed reading about it in public. Would anyone connect me to the disorder if they saw me reading about it? My pulse raced and my stomach churned! By the time I saw the doctor I was a nervous wreck, feeling that "bulimia" was written all over my face and body. Surely I would be found out. But I wasn't!

I made it through the examination, lying about the routine question for my case history—frequent vomiting? I said, "No!" I rationalized that the doctor was questioning about an illness, allergy, or sensitivity, and my vomiting fitted none of those. My secret was still safe.

When I arrived home, I immediately looked up *bulimia* in the dictionary. Was that disgusting word in there? Yes! My only hope was that no one would make the connection between my excessive eating and this word that was now appearing in print. Up until this time I felt I could possibly be the only person ever to practice this behavior, that it was my own discovery. I suspected no one else of bulimia—I guess they were as good at hiding as I was, because now I know that my eating disorder was not unique. Even though I felt alone, I was not! But I had no way of knowing that. All bulimics feel alone and unique.

As eating disorders became more widely publicized, I found I had to bury myself further into food and secrecy. I really had to be careful. I made sure I did not eat too much in front of people. It is hard to believe that I could even know as a bulimic how much was too much! As careful as I tried to be, I still slipped up, especially at big family dinners such as Thanksgiving. I definitely had eaten too much when I had to leave the table to vomit, only to return to eat more. But I was safe. No one noticed, and no one questioned. It saved me from lying again and making excuses. It never occurred to me that discovery might be the only thing that could save me from my illness. I recognized that I was sick, but not sick enough to seek or accept help.

Chapter Two

A Permanent Prison

Many times during my twenty-five years of enslavement to bulimia, I thought I knew what it would take to stop my gorging and vomiting. I had no idea just how "hooked" I was until I tried to stop. But I always had an illusion that a certain something or someone would be the answer.

The first time I vomited, I knew it should be the last time. It was so disgusting, I couldn't imagine repeating it, but I did. I hated bending over the toilet. It was so degrading.

Could there be another way? Maybe if I could think of another place to vomit, I wouldn't do it as often—or better yet, I could quit. Somehow I thought changing the scenery from the inside of a toilet to the inside of a sink might make a difference. So instead of hanging my head in the toilet, I slung it over the sink. Big mistake combined with a big mess! The only advantage was I didn't have to flush the toilet as often, so other people would not be as suspicious about what I was doing in the bathroom. But the disadvantage of cleaning the sink and getting rid of the odors proved too time consuming and risky. Consequently I returned to the toilet to deposit my uncontrollable secret.

The second time I thought I could quit was when I arrived on Western Michigan University's campus. I was convinced a change of address and living quarters would be just the atmosphere I needed to bring my bulimia under control.

As a freshman away from home for the first time, I was free to make my own choices. One of the first choices I wanted to make was to eat like a normal person. Unfortunately, all the food displayed daily in the cafeteria proved to be more than I could handle. In reality my only choice was to take it all in as big a portion as I was allowed. So I continued to vomit breakfast, lunch, and dinner. (Not to mention the many times in between.) So much for the illusion that college would make a difference in my compulsive eating. On the contrary, it proved to be just the atmosphere to maintain the secrecy.

I became extremely thin—just 117 pounds, the thinnest my eating disorder would take me. The pressures and stress of college life were taking an ominous toll on my body. I was living in a whirlwind of classes, vomiting, studying, vomiting, tests, vomiting, papers, vomiting. Vomiting was the period at the end of everything I did. I became physically ill with a strep infection.

This strep actually stopped the downward spiral of my weight loss. It proved to be advantageous for two reasons: One, it scared me. I realized my defenses to attack infection were running dangerously low. I didn't want to die. And, two, had I gotten any thinner I would have been found out! So I took my medicine, got well, and made sure when I vomited I didn't vomit *everything* out. As a result I gained some weight, enough to keep me healthy and pass the scrutiny of anyone who might notice or question my weight. My secret was secure.

The third time I was sure I could quit was when alcohol entered my life. I started to drink instead of eat. Oh, I didn't stop eating altogether, I just found myself drinking during many of those times I used to eat. Alcohol served to numb my emotional distress and lull me into a fantasy world that existed only under the influence of alcohol.

I didn't have to hide this addiction. I was free to drink and get drunk with my friends. My bulimia didn't stop, but now alcohol moved alongside food to numb and camouflage me. I was playing a menacing game, but I thought I was in control the entire time. It never occurred to me that I was only compounding my addictive behavior with the acceptable drug of alcohol.

I dated a lot in college, but I never allowed anyone to get too close. Dating became easier when I started drinking. Drinking was a practical form of socializing. It allowed me to temporarily escape the bondage of food and hide in the mindless effects of alcohol. For a time I could forget my problems and bulimia.

There was nothing like alcohol to postpone the inevitable tumble out of wonderland into the real world. The price was a hangover; a price I was willing to pay for a measure of relief from the stress I was feeling. Alcohol, like food, temporarily filled my spirit, but left me living on empty after the effects wore off. How deluded I was in thinking that switching to alcohol would be the answer.

During those college years I was sure a man and marriage would bring an end to my bulimia. That was the hope I cast as bait before myself to deny how hooked I was. Alcohol had reeled me in as an acceptable way of coping, but I knew the bulimia would have to stop. I was still trapped. Could I ever escape?

How appropriate that John and I met in a bar! It was Happy Hour—that magical time every Friday afternoon when many college students got drunk. And get drunk is what we did every Friday night throughout our courtship and engagement and into marriage. Needless to say, John was not the answer to my accelerating alcohol addiction nor the cure for my bulimia. I had been fooling myself. I couldn't quit. I didn't know how to quit. I was stuck. The "terrible trap" had become my prison.

Both these addictions accompanied me on our wedding day, the one day I had always thought would be the turning point in my life to start down a new path free of any excess baggage that could cripple a relationship. Little did I know just how long this baggage would burden me. If I had any idea it would be for the next twenty years, I'm not sure I would have committed to anything else. My eating disorder required full-time maintenance.

In thinking back on our wedding, it is hard for me to believe that I ate, drank, and vomited my way through the day. It doesn't seem possible that a woman decked out in a full-length white gown could be capable of such distasteful behavior, but I was. This day had no effect on my addictive behaviors; it only served as another occasion to practice them under the disguise of a celebration.

After our wedding I had it in the back of my mind that pregnancy would be the time when I would give up these addictions for good. I had learned to manage my marriage and addictions very nicely. I certainly didn't want to rush into anything that could upset my drinking, eating, and vomiting cycle. So I used pregnancy as the next bait for quitting. But I wanted to postpone pregnancy as long as possible.

As with everything else so far, pregnancy had no effect on my eating disorder or alcohol consumption. I was fooling myself into thinking it would. I simply moved into this phase of my life as I did the others—in total denial that my addictive behaviors were a problem. I was always looking forward to that time in the future when I would quit, baiting myself into further secrecy and deception. So far I had made every necessary adjustment in life for my secret to survive, and I was confident I could continue to do so.

After Jeff was born, we moved into our first home. With the excitement and adrenaline rush of moving, I was positive these addictions would just fall by the wayside. I was looking forward to starting over, and I thought a new home and neighborhood would be just the incentive I needed. It didn't take long for the newness to wear off.

We settled in easily, and I fell back into the old patterns of eating and drinking. Actually, there had never been much of a shift in the old patterns. Nothing had changed. My eating disorder, fueled with alcohol, went full-steam ahead.

The longer I perpetuated my bulimia, the more creative

and committed I became to it. Now I am amazed to see how twisted my thinking became to keep my secret.

Moving into our new home was a perfect example of this. I had left the security of our apartment, where we were hooked up to city sewers. In our new home we were on a septic system. This could definitely pose a problem for someone who was continually filling a toilet with vomit. Was it possible to fill a septic tank?

I decided it probably was. Why didn't I think of this before we moved? It was the denial. I was so sure this move would be what I needed to bring my six-year addictive cycle to an end. It was too painful to think of the consequence beforehand. I wanted to be "normal." Marriage, children, and a home were "normal." But my thinking process and behavior were unfavorably "abnormal." How paranoid I was to think anyone else would figure out my secrets. It would require them to think the way I did. I was a fool to think that was possible!

The only solution I could conjure up for the vomit that was rapidly filling our septic tank was to get rid of it elsewhere. Could I bury it? Yes. Could I haul it to another disposal site? Yes. Could I disguise it in my garbage can? Yes. Was I desperate? Yes.

This was absolutely crazy. Someone would have to be as paranoid as I was to figure this out. And I thought someone might! Incredible!

I don't know how long I continued that desperate disposal act. It just finally became too much to handle — quite literally. I resorted to having the septic tank pumped annually. Why didn't I think of that sooner?

Obviously, maintaining my eating disorder required a lot of skill. It also required masking a lot of panicky feelings. I don't know what panicked me more — not having food available to eat or not having a place to vomit after I ate it. Both required me to be in control. The urge to eat was constant. Keeping food close by was a necessity. I would become jittery and anxious when it was not readily available. I tried to avoid those situations, but that was not always possible.

Many times I would just have to wait it out, or use the children as an excuse to get food to fill my emptiness.

Likewise, to have eaten and have no place to vomit set off a rush of uncontrollable urges. A prime spot for this to happen was after eating in the car. I'd want to scream, "Stop the car!" so I could vomit on the side of the road. It required a lot of forethought and planning to avoid situations where a toilet wouldn't be at my disposal.

Food and alcohol were my partners in addiction during those early years of marriage and child-rearing. There were times I switched back and forth between the two, but I never left food for very long. Alcohol served as a parenthesis to numb my pain and keep my vulnerability hidden. It was an excuse to let go and forget my secret. But I always returned to the secrecy of food. The alcohol addiction exhausted itself after nine years, but the food addiction continued for another fifteen years.

The Addictive Cycle

The addictive cycle took over my life. I never realized how insidious it was until I had escaped it. In the midst of the battle, it was totally unrecognizable. But it ran its course many times daily for twenty-five years.

The trigger for me to eat didn't necessarily have to be something bad or stressful. In college, stress seemed to be the primary cause, but as I got older any feelings, positive or negative, could trip my mind into thinking about food as a means for enduring life.

Food lingered in my subconscious thoughts as the answer to all feelings and situations. It was tucked safely away and ready to comfort me when feelings began to surface. Food was my security blanket—consoling, covering, and calming.

I didn't even have to be aware of what I was feeling. I just reached for food. To go without it would start a wave of panic. In college, I stole food to keep from drowning under these panicky feelings. As I got older, I was able to finesse them better by making sure food was available upon demand.

There was no way I could stop myself once I felt that panic. I had to eat. If I was in the car, I would stop at the nearest fast-food restaurant—sometimes I would skip from one to another until I was full or the intense urge to eat was bridled. While in a grocery store, I could buy whatever I needed and begin my feast in the car on the way home. At home I would leave a room full of people to indulge myself in the kitchen. Nothing short of the unavailability of food could stop me, so I made sure I had food even if I had to leave the house to go buy it.

How long I indulged myself in these binges depended on several variables: time, people, place, and the amount of food available. If I was home alone during the day, there was no pressure. I could take my time, repeating the cycle as necessary or until the food ran out and I had to buy more. If I was alone in the car, I had to finish before arriving home. This could be accomplished by taking detours along the way or driving slowly. The point is, once I started there was no stopping. Binging became a ritual I repeated many times daily.

After each binge it was necessary for me to purge through vomiting. I could find no way to stop this either; it was part of the ritual. Only after I had eaten and vomited until I was empty, did guilt, remorse, and shame set in. How long the guilt remained depended on how rapidly I could rationalize the consequences. For twenty-five years my secret was safe, so I rationalized quickly. Discovery was the worst consequence I could think of, and that never happened.

As a result I moved swiftly from guilt and shame into denial. A large part of my denial was thinking I could stop whenever I wanted. I made false promises never to binge and purge again. I took a measure of solace in those thoughts even though I knew they were void of any truth.

I wish I could say my eating disorder disrupted a normal schedule once a day or once a week, but in reality I repeated this binging-and-purging cycle as many as twenty or more times a day. I could move from the initial thought to the actual binge in a matter of seconds. Once denial set in I was primed to start over.

It is hard to believe I did all of this as a wife and a mother. But I did. Jeff and Jenny grew accustomed to my habits. I don't believe they could sense anything was wrong. I did much of my binging and purging alone, and food did the job of covering my pain. Consequently I gave no visible clues. As with most people, the children really didn't know what to look for.

John could sense that something was not right with me, but he could never quite put it all together. He was caught up in his world of teaching and coaching, and I put on the mask of being capable of handling anything. As long as I was in command, I felt confident I wouldn't get caught. I kept John out of the kitchen and away from the food budget. I used my anger and manipulation to keep things under control. I was a master-manipulator—my self-protection depended on it. Even though I was out of whack, I kept things on an even keel in the home. As long as people didn't mess with my food, I managed to keep the household balanced.

John was not totally ignorant of my struggle. He had no clue what the struggle was, but he knew one existed. This became evident one day two years before I first started counseling. We were having a discussion about how I spoke to the children. I had been overly harsh and angry with them. Evidently this was a pattern John had noticed before, and he brought it to my attention. I felt guilty and threatened because I knew he was right. The children were marching to the rhythm of my angry drum, a drum that beat loudly and startled them into obedience. What else could I do? I felt defensive.

John said many things during our talk that I don't remember. But there was one comment I've never forgotten. He looked at me and simply said, "Mary, every now and then I get a glimpse of a soft woman underneath that hard exterior. I would love to get to know her. I wish Jeff and Jenny could see more of her too."

Those words gave me hope. I desperately wanted more of that softness. John could actually see it—it must be there.

Was that possible? So far everything coming out of me seemed angry, repulsive, and hard. I wanted to know. I was ready to see just what could be required to become the soft woman John desired me to be.

The Shame of It All

It never occurred to me that shame would rear its contemptuous head as I wrote this chapter. Somehow I thought I had left it behind. But when I reread what I had written, I realized shame and contempt were very evident. Both needed to be addressed as a part of recovery.

Dan Allender's book, *The Wounded Heart* (NavPress, 1990), has been most valuable to me in figuring out this process of recovery. I found it helpful to see shame described as "an excellent path to exposing how we really feel about ourselves, what we demand of ourselves and others, and where we believe life can be found. It unearths the strategies we use to deal with a world that is not under our control" (Allender, 53). Ironically enough, even though I was writing about my past, I needed to recover from the shame this particular chapter evoked in the present. I knew sooner or later I would have to expose those ugly secrets and thought patterns, but I assumed I could "just do it" to get my point across. It never occurred to me that I would find myself ensnared in renewed shame and contempt.

The week I wrote this was a terrible one. I was really struggling. By the time I recognized the struggle, I was reduced to tears of shame. All I could get on paper were degrading and distasteful words. Yet when I tried to pray, I could find no words to express myself. A part of me was choking over what I had exposed and what I still could not articulate. (Just writing about shame caused my cheeks to flush and get warm. My body grew sweaty as the cold November winds blew outside.)

As I thought about how I "slung" my head in the sink, was "decked out" in white, and how "twisted" my thinking had become, I just wanted to hide and forget this whole project. My words were working against me as I felt "baited, deluded, fooled, trapped, bridled, and desperate." Were those really my words? Did they describe me? Surely if this depraved soul of mine is ever revealed, no one will ever enjoy my presence again. Whom can I trust with this chapter? So far I had trusted no one with any of these written words, not even John.

As a result I found myself avoiding him. Throughout the week I was dodging his eyes and his presence. Any form of physical intimacy with John was out of the question. I was sure he would understand if he knew the shameful secrets I was writing about.

In my shame I wanted to bury, disguise, and haul myself away, just like my vomit. I felt no better. What could I do with all this?

I viewed myself with contempt. Dan Allender describes contempt as being "absurd in that it inevitably increases man's vulnerability while it enables him to regain a semblance of control that protects him against dependence on God. Contempt is a major weapon against the humbling work of God. . . . Contempt is condemnation, an attack against the perceived cause of the shame" (61).

Mentally I began to beat myself up for not being able to pray. Contempt reenforced my distance from John and justified my hardness toward him. It deadened my need for God, and it certainly kept me from looking at the real problem — sin. Now what?

All this seemed pretty legitimate to me, but I knew it was only a charade to keep me from feeling the longings being aroused in my soul — the longing for my husband to know and love me as a woman, and especially as the soft woman who is becoming more visible and, because visible, vulnerable.

In the midst of the tears I did find God. He ministered to me through hymns and choruses. I began to sing "Great is Thy Faithfulness" and "He is Lord" when I could not put words to my prayers. Only after the reassuring effects of those songs could I ask His forgiveness for believing the distorted lies causing me to sin against Him and John. God filled me with His strength to face the exposure and John as a soft and vulnerable woman.

Yes, I did write those words and they were about me. They speak truth about where I have been, and they did produce shame and contempt on this day. But I am thankful those words no longer squeeze me in their shameful grip. Their bondage has been broken.

I have experienced God's presence in a new and powerful way. I realize no one can disgrace the woman He is awakening in me. My reputation rests in Him. "If God is for us, who can be against us?" (Romans 8:31)

Chapter Three

The Struggle with Intimacy

People have asked how I could go through twenty-five years with this eating disorder and manage to get married, go through pregnancy, and raise children. Millions of other women who attempt this same juggling act find it saps their emotions and energy, consequently robbing their families of intimate relationships.

I did not choose to become pregnant, but ten months after we were married I found myself with child. At first I could not figure out what was wrong with me. A skipped period was nothing new; I had skipped before. I had no morning sickness, although I am not sure I could tell because I was vomiting anyway! I put off going to the doctor until I was close to four months along. Then I went to find out what was wrong. Being pregnant didn't surprise me, but made me very apprehensive. I worried about the baby's health, knowing my bulimia was in full force.

My doctor invited me into his study after my exam, and asked me an unusual question: "Are you *really* married?" I was shocked to think he thought I could be lying! "Of course, I am!" was my sharp reply, "Why do you ask?" He went into a long explanation about how *most* married women come to his office for a pregnancy test after their first skipped period. It was very extraordinary to see a married woman already four months along on her first visit. I had no explanation. I just wanted to get out of there. Could he guess I was hiding something?

Each monthly visit to the doctor's office became a dreaded appointment because I was consumed with fear of discovery. On one hand I worried about putting on too much weight; on the other, had I put on enough? Was there anything about my physical condition that would reveal my secret? I was so anxious about these appointments that when they were over I would gorge myself all the way home, stopping at fast food restaurants or eating candy bars. Of course, I would vomit immediately on my arrival home, only to start the cycle over again. My bulimia was the force driving me through pregnancy.

I did not feel the pleasures of nurturing myself or the baby growing inside my body. I had no joy in watching my stomach grow to accommodate the new life I was carrying. I felt guilt as my husband and I decorated and furnished a nursery because I was always worried about the baby's health, knowing full well that my bulimia had the power to destroy not only me, but also the baby I was carrying.

My confidence grew as I began to feel life growing inside me and my check-ups proved both me and the baby to be healthy. Was it possible I could pull this off and still have a normal baby? I just waited with anticipation for it to be over so I would not be responsible for a life other than my own. My goal was to get through it, and I hoped the baby would live through it too. I quickly rationalized those fears, however. *My* self-protection came first.

The only real joy I felt was when Jeff was finally born. I had been granted a miracle as I held a healthy baby boy in my arms. He looked perfectly normal. I really don't think I expected anything else. I had once again gotten through another dreadful time; my secret was still hidden and would continue to be.

As I entered my second pregnancy two years later I wasn't as nervous. I had pulled this off once; I could do it again! Jeff, now a toddler, was keeping me busy, but I was not under as much pressure because I was not working outside the home. Jeff accompanied me to many of my doctor's appointments, and likewise joined me in the banquet afterward. Sad to say, my bulimia had not diminished in the least. But I wasn't worried. I could get through this one more time.

In all outward appearances life seemed normal. Our marriage was fine, our children were arriving on schedule, and we had bought a house. I had learned to juggle my energy between raising a family and keeping my secret. Jeff became a real source of pride and comfort to me. He was also safe because he never threatened my secret. Things seemed good as long as I denied myself the truth of my existence—I lived for food!

I tried to do all the right things as a mother and homemaker to keep anyone from suspecting my eating disorder. I prepared, cooked, and served lots of healthy foods for my family. The junk food I hid to eat alone and in secret. Part of the preoccupation of a bulimic is being consumed not only with eating the food, but in preparing it. I always wanted to be in the kitchen around food, sneaking bites here and there. Thus I took on the appearance of being a good homemaker where in reality I was choosing food over relationships. I did not allow my pregnancy to slow me down in the kitchen, and having a family only accelerated and gave credibility to my food preparation.

Jenny wasn't due for another six weeks when my water broke early in December. I wasn't worried, I just wasn't ready. There was lots I wanted to do before her arrival, and with determination I set out to do it all. Jenny was born that evening, but before her birth I sent John to work and to coach his basketball team, get the oil changed in the car, apply furniture polish to my kitchen cabinets, vacuum all the carpets, do all the laundry, and fix pig hocks and sauerkraut for dinner! I was, once again, totally denying what was happening in my body. It was more important for me to have everything look right and seem to be in complete control than to care for my physical health as well as the baby's.

I never did get to eat those pig hocks and sauerkraut. It wasn't because I didn't want to; John wouldn't let me! The baby was coming and he knew it, even though I was sure there was time to sit down and eat. It seemed so wasteful to let that food go untouched. I really wanted to eat and felt there would still be time to vomit before the birth. It is startling for me now to look back and see how very out of touch I was with reality in my life. I was even denying the pain of labor!

John got me to the hospital just in time! Jenny was born one half hour after our arrival. She was perfect, beautiful, but weighed only five pounds, eight ounces. This was considered the top weight of a premature baby. Jenny had arrived prematurely, but she checked out normal.

Another miracle? I believe so. My placenta had dried up, and Jenny had ceased to get nourishment. Her only hope for survival was to be born. It wasn't until years later that I allowed myself to think that my eating disorder may have been the reason my placenta dried up. Of course no one ever knew I was thinking that. I was still hiding the bulimia, along with my shame and guilt. Denial was my survival!

Jenny's Questions

Over the past sixteen years one of the biggest worries I have had about my bulimia was that my daughter would follow in my footsteps. It became evident very soon that Jenny was not built like I am. I'm tall, thin, and straight up and down —but Jenny is shorter, softer, and built with more curves.

As a pre-teen, Jenny became inquisitive when she noticed my thinness in proportion to what I ate compared with her more rounded shapeliness and the portions she ate. She used to watch me make frequent trips to the bathroom after eating, and she would sometimes stand outside the bathroom door and listen. I had a great gag reflex and could vomit without retching or making any noise. So it wasn't so much what she heard through the closed door that stirred her suspicion, but what she observed when I came out. She could see my red face, my watering eyes, and vomitus on my upper lip. She began to ask if I had thrown up. I looked her straight in the eye and lied, saying, "Of course not!" I excused my appearance by claiming I had coughed or sneezed.

Internally I was horrified! She was the only person ever to question me about vomiting and I lied. At the time, lying to Jenny seemed safer and easier than dealing with the consequences of discovery. I denied that I had stooped to the level of deceiving my daughter and leading her to believe her thinking and observations were not valid. Justifying myself, I decided I would have to be more careful, especially around Jenny, so it would not happen again. Unfortunately, it did happen several more times, and I continued to lie.

As Jenny developed into a young woman, I could see her scrutinizing my body in comparison to her own. She tried to figure out how I stayed so thin even though I ate so much. It is not unusual for daughters to want to be like their mothers, and Jenny was no exception. She wanted to look like me. I became very anxious as I tried to explain to her the differences in our figures, knowing the whole time that I was a fraud. It haunted me that Jenny might resort to bulimia as a way of controlling her body image. I was afraid that if she did, I would be forced to examine my own eating disorder. I used to wonder how I could force *her* into recovery without jeopardizing my *own* damaging behavior.

When I think about this now, I realize I was sicker than I thought. Even though I was deeply concerned that my daughter might imitate me, I was even more dedicated to my own secrecy and food procurement. I just went further into denial and prayed she would never start so that I would never have to stop.

Family Time

During my eating disorder I knew I was struggling with intimate relationships. I wanted intimacy, yet I avoided it. Food had become my partner. It wasn't until I came out of my eating disorder that I began to see what was required of me to become intimately involved with my family, and John in particular.

For years I used food to anesthetize my involvement with them. One pattern that repeated itself was the afternoon snack. As a school teacher, John would arrive home at the same time as Jeff and Jenny. Everyone was hungry and headed for the refrigerator. I tolerated those invasions into my domain by taking charge of preparing whatever was available to eat and eating along with them. It gave me a slight edge to be in control of the food, and the busyness kept me from getting too involved.

It was supposed to be a fun time as everyone shared their day, but I used food to insulate me from getting too emotionally wrapped up in my family's world. Likewise, food was my protection from anyone getting too close to mine.

After the snack John went to do yard work, the children ran to play, and I finished up the leftovers, cleaned up the mess, and threw up the snack. What a relief! My world of secrecy was still intact.

This pattern went on for several years. It should have gotten easier with practice, but in reality it became harder. As the children grew older, they were actively involved in athletics. At snack time I was alone or with only John. Alone was all right—no threat. But when John was with me, I found myself agitated and felt under surveillance. John did nothing to make me feel this way. Just his entrance into our home and kitchen caused those feelings to surface.

In the past the children had served as a buffer to our conversation. Now there were no children. John could focus on me. Could he see my discomfort? Or feel my agitation? I felt scared and out of control. Food was definitely my salvation to this time alone with John. It took every ounce of my being to stay with him and keep the conversation flowing. How much easier it was when the children were present! No amount of practice softened the threat I felt during this time alone with him. It was something I simply endured to keep my secret safe.

Marital Closeness

A lot has changed since I have come out of my eating disorder, but one thing has not—John still comes home every day after work. One might think that now my secret is out, this would no longer be a problem. Wrong! I still feel threatened, but not in being found out. I still get agitated, but not because I am hiding. Those feelings surface because of the burden I feel in being known as a woman.

At times John feels like the enemy invading my territory, and I struggle to let him in. Food no longer serves as my protection to keep him at bay. Food no longer numbs the raw edge of my vulnerability as I become emotionally involved with who he is and who I am. Sometimes I just want to run and hide, but there is nowhere to go. Food is no longer my hiding place.

So what do I do? On a good day I am there for John. I don't put any undue pressure on myself to be all things for him. It is OK for me to sit and listen without feeling I have to have all the answers or right responses. John enjoys me. My physical and emotional presence are what he desires. How simple it all really is! I am enough.

On a bad day I shut him out. Not with food, but with a cold shoulder, a novel in front of my face, or a look that says, "Stay away." Does it work? Sometimes. Other times John moves toward me in his strength to embrace my hurt and pain. How does that feel? Weak—needy—known—loved. Feelings that scare me because I have spent a lifetime struggling to be strong, self-sufficient, hidden, and alone.

John and I are still testing the ground of learning to live openly and honestly with one another. We fail each other daily, but we no longer use our failures as a score card for who is right or wrong. Instead we view those failures as a signal for us to embrace our hurts and frustrations.

It is good to know that after twenty-five years of marriage John and I are capable of change. By the goodness of God we have been able to see it is necessary, and it is by His grace we have been able to do it. We are no longer living in the comfort zone. We are moving out, taking a risk, and trusting God as we look to Him to love one another better.

Sexuality

Loving John better has required me to look at my sexuality as a woman. The sexual abuse I suffered as a child made physical intimacy difficult for me. My eating disorder only "piggy backed" onto the sexual abuse to help me hide my sexuality from John. But even women who have not been sexually abused find that eating disorders disrupt God's plan for the proper expression of their sexuality.

Our bedroom became a battleground as I fought against the numbing effects of food and the stirring sense of my sexuality that simmered just beneath the surface. To give in to these sensual stirrings uncovered feelings of inadequacy, fear of rejection, a loss of control, and images of harlotry. Each one of these had the potential of ruining sex with John. Any combination of the four ended the encounter before it even got started. So how did I function?

Good question! On this side of recovery I've wondered about that many times. It has been very helpful for me to understand how God designed me to be as a sexual woman, and to see how that design was sabotaged by food.

In the sexual relationship God designed me to be open, inviting, responsive, warm, and surrounding. Food and painful memories sabotaged this design for me. I know John was not fully aware of this treason because I was able to function physically. But psychologically and emotionally, I needed food to numb the fear and the shame of being known as a woman. Consequently a binge and a purge usually preceded or precluded a sexual encounter to deaden my emotional turmoil.

At times my body felt like the enemy, betraying me with a sexual response. My body could be open and receiving, but my mind would be closed, distant, isolated or angry. John was getting parts of me, but not the whole woman. Food served as my buffer for sexual intimacy.

For years I entered our bedroom unsure of myself. I felt my body was not desirable or good enough. I worried about my performance and feared that I would be rejected. I was afraid of what sex might awaken within my soul. I was afraid of being out of control. Only food could calm the inside while the outside participated in a controlled level of pleasure.

On this side of recovery I still struggle with the bedroom. It is no longer a battleground, but a certain level of tension still permeates the initial embrace of the encounter. The tension is in being known as a sexual woman, a longing God has awakened in my soul. Trusting God with my sexuality is an ongoing process. I very much want to be known sexually by John, but sexuality excites feelings so unfamiliar to me. Yet I have taken the risk in being known.

Since food no longer serves as my emotional buffer, I've turned to God. I've needed to believe what God says about who I am, "fearfully and wonderfully made," and that He is intimately acquainted with all parts of me. I've had to trust and believe God when He says, "Let marriage be held in honor among all, and let the marriage bed be undefiled" (Hebrews 13:4). Not only is the marriage bed honorable, but so am I.

As I've trusted God with this area of my life, I have been able to approach our bed as a woman free to love and give all parts of myself. I no longer want to be a prisoner of my own sexuality, but free to be intimately known by John. It is possible for me to be open, known, and seen as I willingly give to John the gift of my womanhood. God has honored our bedroom as I have trusted Him with my fears and shame of being a sexual woman. Food no longer stands between me and John, and I'm finding John to be more satisfying and safer than food ever was.

Regrets

As I look back on this period of my life, I feel sadness and regret. It is hard for me to realize that I was actually the woman I am writing about. I feel sorrowful over the lost memories that are meant to bring joy, love, and togetherness in relationships. I feel regret that I was trapped in a compulsive behavior that ruled my very existence. I was running away from life as I put distance between all who knew me, especially those who longed to get close to me and were designed to have a relationship with me.

I grieve that I had to hide the woman in me because who I was would not have been good enough and did not measure up. It is sad to think I deadened feelings of nurture, love, and all that I could have offered by being vulnerable, open, soft, and honest. I denied myself feeling anything that would awaken emotional life in me, whether it be joy or sorrow. I regret that I chose food to mask my life instead of to sustain it as it was designed to. If only I had used my energy to build up relationships instead of keeping my secret.

Still, it is good for me to connect with the woman I was, for it gives me hope and joy to know that I still have time and energy to restore those who have been lost to me, and to give of myself as a caring woman, capable of loving freely as I expose myself honestly.

Chapter Four

Satisfying the Emptiness

My recovery started when I received Jesus Christ as my personal Savior. I had no hope that my bulimia would stop when I made this commitment to Christ. I don't believe I gave it any thought as I prayed. This disorder had consumed my life for ten years, and I did not think there was any help for me. I am not sure I was even looking for help; I simply responded to a message I heard for the first time.

As a young girl I attended church regularly. My mother thought church was important and made sure all three of her children went. I appeared to be the only one of the three where church seemed to "take." I felt a need to atone for being a girl. My brothers were boys and therefore complete in their maleness. I felt that as a girl I didn't quite measure up. Maybe church would be just the thing to bring me up to par.

As a teen I taught younger children in Sunday School and daily Vacation Bible School. One summer I was the song leader, of all things. I couldn't carry a tune, but I was the best they had and I was willing to do it. As a Sunday School teacher I wasn't a whole lot more skilled. On one particular Sunday I remember bringing a *Time* magazine to class and reading a generic Christmas prayer from the inside cover. I knew absolutely *nothing* about prayer or the Bible, short of the Lord's Prayer and the Twenty-third Psalm. It didn't matter that I hadn't a clue where they could be found in the Bible—I just memorized them from a sheet of paper. The saddest part of all this was that I was considered "quality" by the Sunday School superintendent.

So much for my "religious" training. It all came to a screeching halt when I went to college. The once "religious" girl left the church behind and proceeded to fend for herself. I never found the atonement I was looking for. And it never occurred to me to seek the church's help with my bulimia. By this time I was fully enmeshed in the disorder and totally committed to secrecy.

Nothing "religious" entered my life until John and I were married in the church. In 1969 that was the "appropriate" thing to do, and we did it. John and I exited the church after the ceremony, not to reenter until we had Jeffrey baptized two years later. Again that seemed the appropriate thing to do. I, especially, was committed to keeping up the front of doing the "right" thing. It certainly was a smoke screen for my eating disorder, which I knew was totally inappropriate!

John and I "tried" church a few times as the children got older. Again it was the right thing to do; still, religion did not "take." Skipping one Sunday led to skipping the next, and so it went.

In 1976 a major evangelism campaign called "I Found It" swept the United States. The prayers of the people involved and committed to that campaign had to be responsible for my responding to the message of salvation through Jesus Christ. There is no other way I can explain why I agreed to allow a complete stranger to read Scripture to me over the telephone. On top of that, I was able to explain back to her what those Scriptures meant.

For the first time, I really heard John 3:16, "For God so loved the world, that He gave His only begotten Son, that whoever believes in Him should not perish, but have eternal life." I told my telephone "evangelist" that I knew that meant God had given the best He had in His only Son, and all I needed to do was to believe in Him for eternal life.

The second verse the caller read to me was from Romans 5:8: "But God demonstrates His own love toward us, in that while we were yet sinners, Christ died for us." The caller asked what I thought this verse meant. I knew in a moment that it meant God's love was so great that, even though I was a sinner, He still sent His Son to die for me. At this point I was feeling cocky. I was two for two, and on a pretty good roll—ask me anything!

Next the caller read from Romans 3:23: "For all have sinned and fall short of the glory of God." For the first time in my life I recognized that I was a sinner. In the church where I grew up no one talked about *sin*, much less sinners! I had never made the connection that anything I did was wrong or bad, and certainly would not have put it in the category of sin. Startling!

The last verse she read to me was from 1 John 1:9: "If we confess our sins, He is faithful and righteous to forgive us our sins and to cleanse us from all unrighteousness." That one seemed easy. All I had to do was confess my sins, and I would be all right. The caller explained that was correct, *if* I was a child of God. God was not obligated to forgive just anyone. Only those who had received His Son, Jesus Christ, would have God's forgiveness. She asked, "Would you like to pray to receive Jesus Christ as your personal Savior, and have God's forgiveness and *know* you have eternal life?"

I replied, "No."

That had to be the most ridiculous question I had ever been asked. I had *never* prayed with anyone over the telephone. I had *never* heard of such a thing and couldn't believe it. It was definitely time to get rid of this fanatic. But not before she asked if someone could make a follow-up call the next day. For reasons known only to God, I said, "Yes!"

That proved to be the most important telephone call I was ever to receive! And the follow-up visit proved to be the most important one I would ever have! I wanted to avoid the follow-up all together, but God's timing was perfect in that I *was* home to receive the caller. I wish I could say I welcomed her into my home, but I did not! I was rude and angry that she had caught me there.

On top of that she looked the role of what I had come to see as typical of a religious person. No makeup, wire-rimmed glasses, a head scarf, an old corduroy coat, and orthopedic shoes. I didn't want her in my house, but my anger turned to curiosity as she undauntedly proceeded to ask, "Are you a Christian?"

"Of course I am! I was raised in a church, and I am a citizen of the United States," was my confident reply. The whole time I was thinking that if being a Christian meant looking like her, I wanted no part of it!

"Do you know you would go to heaven if you were to die tonight?" she questioned with a grin on her face. How could she be smiling? I wasn't.

"I believe I would stand a good chance of getting there. I've never done anything really bad, and I know others who are worse off than me, so surely I would go to heaven. Doesn't everyone? All my friends believe they will go to heaven. We couldn't all be wrong, could we?" She was starting to get under my skin. By this time my curiosity had turned to visible hostility that obviously wasn't throwing her off course.

She never answered my questions, she only asked, "Do you have a personal relationship with Jesus Christ?"

I was stumped! No one had ever asked me that. My interest was stirred. "I have never heard of that before. How would I know if I have a personal relationship with Jesus Christ?"

The grin turned into a broad smile that made her eyes sparkle behind those wire-rimmed glasses as she confidently said, "Oh, you'd know it if you have a personal relationship with Jesus Christ!" Clearly, this lady knew something I didn't, and I wanted to know what it was.

My countenance relaxed as I tried to become more welcoming. I had some hostile ground to recover and hoped she wouldn't hold it against me. She was running late, but she left a booklet for me to read, and I, as kindly as I was capable of, asked her to return. I was swept with relief when she agreed to come back the next day. What a sacrifice for her, considering that was the day before Thanksgiving!

That night I read the booklet, which contained the verses I had heard over the phone plus a few more. When the woman returned, I had a question concerning the word "received" in John 1:12: "But as many as received Him, to them He gave the right to become children of God, even to those who believe in His name." I didn't get it! It was very clear I needed to do something, but what was it? My caller said the "something" was to pray, and she asked if I would like to pray to receive Jesus Christ as my personal Savior. I didn't hesitate to say yes.

It was a simple prayer. "Lord Jesus, I need You. Thank You for dying on the cross for my sins. I open the door of my life and receive You as my Savior and Lord. Thank You for forgiving my sins and giving me eternal life. Take control of my life, Make me the kind of person You want me to be." No angel placed a halo on my head, I heard no bells ringing, but I knew I had made the most important decision of my life.

This lady became a very dear friend as she discipled me for the next six months. My focus went beyond what she looked like as I began to see her heart. It proved to be one committed to Christ and dedicated to grounding me, as a new believer, in Him. She stayed close to me for years to come—but I still held her at a distance to protect my secret.

I wish I could say all my earthly problems were solved in that prayer, but they were not. The new road I was starting down proved to have many detours. But it was a start. As for my bulimia, it was still there driving me to even further secrecy, especially now as a Christian. What would I ever do if anyone found me out?

How arrogant I was to think that God had not found me out! My arrogance carried me through the next fifteen years of secrecy and hiding from Him. But God proved to be patient and long-suffering during those years. When I finally turned from food to Him, He was there to embrace me and fill the spirit that had been living on empty.

Answered Prayer

God is true to His Word, and He began to work in my life. The very day I received Christ He began to convict me of sin. Until then I had never considered my language offensive. In college I had picked up every four-letter word circulating throughout campus. I was able to incorporate them into my vocabulary with ease and impact. After receiving Christ, I was horrified at the mere sound of them coming from my mouth or the mouths of others. I knew I could do nothing about the others, but I could do something about myself.

As fluent as I was with words, I was tongue-tied when it came to prayer. How could I pray about my language? I hadn't even started to read the Bible; I knew nothing. In my first feeble attempt at prayer I asked, "God, take those words from my mouth. I don't want them there any longer."

God ultimately honored that prayer, but I faced my first realization of how ingrained my sin was. As much as I wanted to get rid of those words, still a few were slipping past my lips daily. Gradually they didn't come out at all. It took two weeks. Unfortunately, I still battle with those words in my mind, but at least they don't get past my lips. Somehow I thought it would be easy, but I discovered that bridling my tongue was tough. It felt good to go through my first day with not one of those words in my conversation. I felt clean. Granted, it was a small victory, but one I needed to see the faithfulness of God to answer prayer.

The Juggling Act: Alcohol and Food

As much as I enjoyed Bible study and fellowship, I was not fully convinced that Christians could have fun. Even though

God was making changes in my life, I still wanted to hang onto the things I felt I needed to really enjoy life. Of course, food, coupled with alcohol, was one of those things.

I refused to talk about my eating disorder with anyone, including God. So binging and purging continued to be my secret. Ironically, my new friends made this part of my life easier. I quickly discovered that much of what they did revolved around food. Food was available at Bible study, at social gatherings at church or in homes, before business meetings, and most any other time we met. Wonderful! I took these opportunities to binge and purge under the disguise of the church. My denial even had me thinking that the food part was fun, but where was the alcohol in all of this?

One thing I learned fast was that these new friends did not drink. In my arrogance I kept it no secret that I did! They would just have to accept the fact I enjoyed drinking. How could someone so vocal about alcohol be so hidden about food? Easy. Alcohol was acceptable by the world's standard, and the eating disorder was not. I could live with that. Alcohol served as a smoke screen to what I was really hiding in my food addiction. No one could see beyond the alcohol to catch my even deeper problem. I felt pretty safe with these people.

I hadn't counted on conviction by the Holy Spirit to begin to take root in my life. In my stubbornness to avoid the Spirit, my alcohol addiction actually got worse. The more I was in God's Word, the worse I felt and the more I drank to numb out His conviction. I was a mess juggling between alcohol and food. Both were taking a toll in my life.

Finally, after a year as a Christian and one very humiliating experience with alcohol when I actually had a blackout, I knew I had gotten out of control. I was overwhelmed with guilt and shame and knew the drinking had to stop. My fun had turned dangerous! I turned to God for help and found it in His Word. I prayed and claimed Psalm 37:5: "Commit your way to the LORD, trust also in Him, and He will do it." I did just that. Once I prayed and gave the addiction to God,

I trusted Him to do something with it. And He did. Alcohol exited my life as quickly and easily as it had entered. The nine-year battle with alcohol was finished.

Sounds too easy? Maybe it was, but I still had food!

My battle with alcohol was finished, but another one was brewing with John. I was his "good time" party girl. Now who would he drink with? He wasn't totally convinced there was life and fun beyond alcohol. After one particularly strained evening at the bar where he drank and I didn't, we had a blowup. It ended in bed, John feeling justified on his side and I feeling righteous on mine—with a chasm between. "You are not the same girl I married, and I prefer the one I married," was all he said. I felt terrible, and for the first time in our seven years of marriage I questioned the security of my position as his wife. Would he find another drinking partner?

No. I just had everyone in Bible study double up on their prayers for John, who still had not committed his life to Christ. Once again I claimed Psalm 37:5 for him and trusted God. Slowly the issue of alcohol lost its steam as we began to redirect our social life to include our children. Many of my new Christian friends helped by inviting us into their homes and including us in their family activities. Even though John liked the girl he had married, he was beginning to see value in the one God was molding. John was willing to give up the bar life, not only for me, but for the witness to our children. In less than two years John committed his life totally to Christ. The prayers of many people had been answered.

Ultimately we found there was life after alcohol, and we've been having fun ever since!

So why couldn't I commit and trust God with food? Certainly God would honor my prayer a third time.

The only explanation I have is that I believed my food addiction was too repulsive and too much for God to handle. I felt I was a dangerous woman, too much for even God. In my arrogance I would not allow Him to enter my eating disorder.

Did I quit the Christian life? No. Did I drop out of Bible study? No. Did I stop praying? No. On the contrary, I went after Christ with as much fervor as ever, still totally denying my binging and purging. I entered the life of a two-faced Christian—committed both to Christ *and* my eating disorder.

The Masterful Hypocrite

I succeeded marvelously as a hypocrite. In my ignorance of the Christian walk, I thought I was the only one playing this hypocritical game. If I really had been, I might have gotten caught, but I had no way of knowing that. It took years for me to realize I wasn't the only Christian committed to secrecy about something in life. But, as happens when we hide, I failed to see the pain and concealment of those around me. I was too focused on my own. No one saw me and I saw no one.

Because of my success as a hypocrite, my healing was postponed for fifteen years. My success at secrecy motivated me to continue my eating disorder. As long as I could masterfully juggle Christ and food without discovery, I had no conviction to quit.

I harbored a lot of guilt as a hypocrite, but I rationalized my guilt along with my eating disorder. The biggest part of rationalizing was denying the existence of the problem. So far I had rationalized away ten years in an eating disorder. Becoming a Christian added a new dimension of guilt over this, but my survival depended on secrecy no matter how guilty I felt. I could handle the guilt, but not the exposure. The guilt was the lesser of the two evils. The key was not to think about it.

So my hypocrisy continued, and so did my cover-up. In all of this I hid from people but was never hidden from God. It wasn't because I wasn't trying, it just was not possible! No one, not even me, could hide from God. He was aware of every move I made, including the despicable ones from the refrigerator to the toilet.

Why did He put up with me for so long? It is because He is a kind and patient God. It was His love and long-suffering that would eventually lead me to repent. Romans 2:4 states, "Or do you think lightly of the riches of His kindness and forbearance and patience, not knowing that the kindness of God leads you to repentance?" God stayed with me even though I thought I was hiding from Him.

My Problem—Too Big for God?

In thinking back over those years, I have asked myself several questions. The answers to these questions did not come all at once, but have unfolded over the years as I look at the recovery process. Because God is "rich in mercy" (Ephesians 2:4), I didn't have to deal with everything at once. His grace was extended to me over and over again, "For of His fullness we have all received, and grace upon grace" (John 1:16). I believe seeing the whole process at once would have been more than I could have handled. Why? Because the process involved my sin. He graciously revealed that to me a little at a time.

Why did I hide so long? Any excuse I give at this point is weak at best, but nonetheless it kept me hiding for fifteen years. At the time I felt no one would understand, not even God. I didn't understand my problem myself, so how could I expect anyone else to? I didn't think there was anyone I could trust with this secret. The longer my secret was kept, the more powerful it became. After ten years it had become jet-propelled beyond anyone's comprehension. And after twenty-five years its grip held me in a vise, squeezing the life out of me. Surely my secret had the power to kill me if it were ever revealed! Thus I tucked it away, wrapped in denial to deal with at a later date. Only after my secret was divulged did it lose its power to grip and control my life.

Why didn't I take it to God sooner? I felt it was too repulsive for Him to handle. Besides, I had lived twenty-eight years without God and still felt there were things I could manage on my own. My eating disorder would stay under my management for another fifteen years.

Could I possibly be the first Christian to be hiding an eating disorder? Possibly so, and I didn't want to shock God with it. What if I took it to Him, and it didn't stop? I had gotten myself into this; I would get myself out. I didn't want any help.

So where was God during those years? He was present with me and allowing me to live. I could not hide from Him. "And there is no creature hidden from His sight, but all things are open and laid bare to the eyes of Him with whom we have to do" (Hebrews 4:13). He was equipping me through the power of His Word to one day face my secret. "For the Word of God is living and active and sharper than any two-edged sword, and piercing as far as the division of soul and spirit, of both joints and marrow, and able to judge the thoughts and intentions of the heart" (Hebrews 4:12). Just because I refused to acknowledge my eating disorder before God didn't mean I couldn't learn and grow from His Word.

The seeds of God's Word were being sown in my life. Some were growing and bearing fruit while others were germinating just under the surface. Those seeds were being watered and kept alive; it was just taking longer for them to sprout. As God's Word progressively shed light on those seeds, they were able to grow. Some seeds took years to sprout, but I firmly believe the germinating process was necessary for me to eventually see my sin. It was my sin that kept those seeds from sprouting in the first place.

God is true to His Word when He says, "So shall My Word be which goes forth from My mouth: It shall not return to Me empty, without accomplishing what I desire, and without succeeding in the matter for which I sent it" (Isaiah 55:11).

It was God's desire that I come to Him with my eating disorder. It was in His Word that I saw my need to approach His throne of grace and seek His forgiveness. If it hadn't been for the Word of God combined with the Spirit of God I might never have come.

The Communion Table: Feast or Famine?

As a Christian on this side of recovery, I still find some of my old thinking patterns hard to shake. It is not unusual for me to come into prayer confessing the sin of my eating disorder even though I am no longer enmeshed in it. It is hard to shake those old habits of confession. I found this to be especially true one Sunday.

As I entered church and saw the Communion table set up, my mind drifted back over years of guilt and shame. The memories surfaced like a tidal wave ready to pull me under as I thought about the numerous times I faced that table. *That* sin was on the tip of my tongue. I began to wonder if I'd ever simply be able to forget those twenty-five years. Or would I be like a robot programmed to confess the same sin over and over?

My immediate reaction was to shake the "negative" thoughts. I just wanted to sit there and enjoy the worship service with my family. But as the organ commenced to play, my thoughts returned to The Sin. So I decided to see why today, in particular, these thoughts seemed to be on my mind so strongly.

As I glanced to my right and left, it didn't take long to see why. Seated with me was my entire family. That in itself may not seem unusual, but with two children away at college, our Sundays together in church are becoming a thing of the past. It felt safe to be sitting with three people who knew about my eating disorder but, more important, *who knew all about me and still loved me!*

Did I really think I wanted to forget those twenty-five years? I don't think so. The Communion table has great significance for Christians as we recognize the broken body and shed blood of Christ, but as a woman fighting an eating disorder it can represent the extremes of the battle.

As an anorexic teenage girl, one small bite of food was too much for me; as a bulimic woman a thousand bites were not enough. Food had the capability to trigger uncontrollable binges or controllable starvation. As I came face to face with the communion table, could I risk the power packed in one small cracker and a sip of juice?

For me the Communion table was not a place of worship. It threatened the secret of my soul as I confessed the sin of my eating disorder and struggled with the mere mechanics of lifting the elements to my mouth. Would the urge to eat it all surface, or would I need to vomit the tiny morsel?

So the battle raged! It wasn't until I came to God *spiritually bankrupt* that peace began to fill my soul. Why did I struggle for so long? I denied that I was hopeless and hooked. God was the only One who could fill my empty spirit and free my soul.

On this particular Sunday it felt good to remember. The tidal wave of guilt and shame had receded. I don't ever want to become complacent about where I've been or lose sight of where I'm going. God has extended His grace to me and my family, and I won't forget it. I no longer confess the sin of my eating disorder to God—that battle is finished! Now the communion table is a place of reconciliation and thanksgiving to be shared with the body of Christ and with my family.

Prodigal Daughter

The practice of binging and purging is so repulsive it is really hard to forget, especially as a Christian. I had been two-faced for so long that at times it seemed to be screaming out of my soul. The practice is damaging and certainly warrants forgetting, but not if it means forgetting my sin against God along with it.

God is certainly good to have even kept me alive, and even more gracious to have put up with the sheer arrogance of my struggle. Like the prodigal son in Luke 15, I was bent on self-indulgence. I wanted my own way, which isolated me from God and proved to be sinful. Sin always breeds separation from God. The price of my sin was costly. I spent my dreams, relationships, health, clear conscience, and friendships. Sin led to self-degradation: binging and purging were very damaging and humiliating. Like the prodigal, I longed to be filled and found no value in the food fit for swine, but I had been willing to settle for it. I needed to come out of the "pig-pen" and return to the Father. Only when my emptiness brought me to true self-awareness did I begin to see my spiritual bankruptcy and think there had to be something better. And transformation came when I returned openly to the Father and admitted my sin against Him.

So what have I learned from the prodigal son? That he and I had a lot in common, both of us seeking fulfillment away from the Father. But, more important, I learned about the character of God. God had been patiently waiting for me and was glad when I finally came to Him. It didn't matter that it took so long (although I'm sure He would have liked me to have come to my senses sooner); He rejoiced when I came. He had compassion and embraced me in my repentance. I found complete love and forgiveness in Him. Only God could fill the emptiness in my soul with spiritual food seasoned with grace and mercy—food that satisfies for eternity.

Chapter Five

Food and Bondage: Darkness, Deception, Deceit

Food held me in bondage and controlled my choices for so many years. In the throes of my eating disorder I knew food was number one, but I never consciously admitted its monopoly on my life. Denial ruled my existence like a dark and heavy curtain drawn across the window of my mind, casting out the light of reality and hope.

Because I was not a Christian for the first ten years of my eating disorder, being in darkness was nothing new. The enemy of my soul had free reign to twist and distort my mind. Satan is an expert in the art of deception, and I learned his ways well. At the time the mere mention of any bond to Satan would have seemed ludicrous. I had no resources to draw upon to recognize the root of my problem. I was simply stuck—just as he wanted me to be.

Satan's first attack on my mind coincided with the evening my father commented to me about getting fat. When I gazed into the mirror to examine my body, I saw fat even though the bathroom scales verified I weighed 150 pounds —not an extreme amount considering I was five feet eight inches tall! My mind distorted my vision so I did not see my true body, which was *not* fat. I saw myself as fat!

So the deception began in spite of the evidence—I had bought into a lie! A lie that could not be dispelled at any cost. Even when I dieted down to 125 pounds, I was not thin enough. I felt I had to stay thin, or I would self-destruct. Yet self-destruct is what I did as I maintained my image through bulimia and vomiting. The chains of bondage choked me and drove me into the secret world of deceit, one that forced hostility to rule in order to guard my secret.

The Hostile Mask

Hostility became my mask to keep others away and out of my life. Craftiness coexisted with hostility as I cleverly protected my secret. Most people did not see the deception because I seasoned my hostility with humor. Much of the time my humor was at the expense of others to deflect anyone from seeing behind my mask. If anyone got too close, I dropped her as my friend.

This happened with Nancy. Ten years ago I made a clean cut in my relationship with her. She had been a close friend and confidant for five years, but she was starting to get nosy about my mask. How did I know that? She confronted me on my hostility and chastised me for my cruel and sarcastic humor. Her words made me even angrier because she was right and there was a genuine measure of concern. Instead of finding comfort in her concern, I became frightened at being found out.

Nancy would not back away as others did. She was getting too close; especially when she gave me a book to read on anger. Ironically enough, that made me furious. Only Satan was capable of ruining and distorting relationships to this point, and I yielded to him. Nancy was dropped!

I have since restored my relationship with Nancy. She was the fifth person I told about my eating disorder. Nancy deserved to know because she had come so close to the heart of my struggle. I came with a cloud of shame hanging over my head for having allowed my hostility and eating disorder to put so much distance between us. Only by the grace of God could Nancy embrace me in my disclosure. I believe

Nancy would have embraced me ten years ago. But I didn't know that and was not willing to risk my exposure. Satan had me believing that she would have dropped me in disgust. His lies kept me hidden, not only from her, but from my family and others for years to come.

How wonderful it has been to have a friend who still values me and can see worth and potential after twenty-five years of destructive behavior. This book was her idea! Her enthusiasm and insight have been my mainstay to remain on course to its completion. Writing my story has helped to heal many memories and relationships. Satan has attempted to stop this process, but too many people have been praying and cheering me on. I would have to say that Nancy has been the main cheerleader, with God the Captain of the squad!

Picture Perfect

Satan truly twisted my mind and thought processes while I was in college. He actually started before I even applied to go. I had many options open to me, but because of my insecurities I felt I had only one: the same college my two older brothers were attending. Somehow I thought they would be my buffer if I couldn't cut it academically, socially, or emotionally. I doubted my ability even to survive. I had no resources to draw upon—I was flooded with the possibility of failure and found myself drowning under the pressure even before I left home. Combine these negative and overwhelming thoughts with my eating disorder, and the enemy had an easy time setting me up for secrecy and control.

No one knew of my insecurities or how I felt. I had mastered this deception throughout my high school career. My eating disorder filled the gap. On the outside I appeared confident, controlled, focused, and outgoing—all the characteristics so admired by my parents and teachers. Combine these characteristics with my drive to be an overachiever, and I was a picture of success. On top of this I had dieted down to a perfect size 8—who could ask for anything more?

Not even my parents could detect my problem. My dad used to say, "The sun rises and sets on Mary Jane." I was everything they ever wanted in a daughter, and in their eyes, I was picture perfect. Somehow who I was got crowded out of this perfect picture. Their comments pressured me further into my mask of hostility and hiding. As a result, I got lost in the picture as I fought to maintain who I thought they wanted me to be.

Those loving words from my parents did not penetrate me for the good of my soul. Satan used them against my already wounded spirit. I have come to realize that only Satan is capable of twisting something intended for good into something bad. I did not know any truth from the Word of God to combat this enemy attack. I had bought into his lies of deception so much that even as a Christian his grip held me for another fifteen years.

Sink or Swim?

Food was controlling so much of my life that I dropped out of activities that had the potential of giving me recognition on campus. One in particular was my selection into the Synchronized Swimming Club. I was excellent in water ballet and had led my high school club for four years. When I tried out for the Club in my freshman year, I was a "shoo-in" on the first round of tryouts. This club would have exposed me to a group of girls I had something in common with, as well as given me the opportunity to exercise my skill, not only as a synchronized swimmer, but as a choreographer in music. It would have been good for me to have an extra-curricular activity and be involved with people in a fun, yet challenging, atmosphere.

Unfortunately, I dropped out of the club almost as quickly as I had been selected into it. I used the excuse that it required time I could not afford to take away from my studies. As I look back, I see that was just a smoke screen for the real reason I quit.

My eating disorder was the real reason. I was too thin, and no matter what the water temperature, I was freezing. My feet, knees, hands, elbows, and lips were always a purplish blue, and I could not stop shaking. The club held practice during the dinner hour, so my dinnertime and food selections would be limited. And I looked terrible in those tank suits. I was just too thin and flat-chested, and I would not risk any scrutiny of my body.

Once again I withdrew from people and into myself to hide. I distanced potential friends and submerged myself under the numbing effects of food. Swimming was no longer fun or important to me. I was drowning in despair, wondering how and why my life had sunk into the depths of hopelessness.

Even though I was sinking, I felt very much in control and *thought* I had made the right choices about college and synchronized swimming. In reality I was too helpless to choose. I was a driven young lady committed to secrecy and deceit, which ruled my choices to a point that rendered me powerless to choose anything else. I had been a player who participated in Satan's game of deception, never even realizing I had been recruited.

Family Gatherings—Then and Now

Family gatherings were always a challenge with my eating disorder. The holidays were the worst, especially Thanksgiving. All that food combined with the pressure to eat consumed my mind and body until I thought they both would explode. In some ways that is exactly what happened: I ate so much and vomited so much that I felt tired and dizzy. It took a lot of energy to fortify my mind with hostility to keep others away. It also took some calculated maneuvering to excuse myself from the table to vomit so I could return to eat more! Those close family times were such a threat to discovery that I was glad when the day ended and everyone was out of my way.

Thanksgiving is different now—thank goodness! Food no

longer holds me in bondage. I am free to prepare, choose, and eat food. It was great freedom for me to sit at a table with my family knowing I could make choices, eat my fill, and fellowship honestly with those who knew me. When my husband asked each one of us what we were thankful for this year, it was a great release for me to say, "I'm thankful to be free to eat and enjoy food with my family. It feels good to be accepted and loved by people who know about my past with food and rejoice in my recovery." I did not feel I had to hide, but was liberated to enjoy all the day had to offer of food, fun, and fellowship.

I remember feeling slightly irritated when I was left to finish the last of the cleanup while everyone went downstairs to play Ping-Pong and pool. I wanted to hurry to be with them. I actually felt I was missing something! How different from before, when I would isolate myself, withdraw from any fun, and linger in the kitchen as long as possible to nibble on leftovers. Ordinarily I would nibble until they were gone; now I don't know what to do with them!

My mind is still on volumes of food even though I'm no longer consuming it in volumes. Will I ever learn to prepare "normal" proportions? Maybe, maybe not. It isn't what really matters any longer. It is just a relief to be able to face food without the compulsion or craving to eat it all.

Two weeks after Thanksgiving I finally had to throw out the remaining leftovers. My family had eaten their full, and so had I. They were even starting to complain about those leftovers; something relatively new for all of us. I tossed them in the garbage. No guilt, no remorse, no longings to retrieve them. God had broken the bondage of Satan's stronghold. It, too, lay in the garbage, never again to be resurrected in my life.

Food Poisoning? Not Me!

The closest I ever came to really being found out was at a family gathering in Tennessee. My husband's family is from the South, and we were visiting there for Easter. John had a relative who had passed away two weeks before our visit, and we found ourselves feasting on the desserts left over from the funeral. Everything was rich, creamy, and home-made. As usual there were too many choices; as usual I couldn't make one, so I took a piece of everything, including a tainted chess pie. Everyone loved that pie, laden with eggs and milk, and firmly packed with fat and calories. We all agreed it tasted delicious. It even tasted relatively good on the way back up as I purged mine in the toilet shortly after eating it.

I was fortunate that I did vomit it up. It saved me a lot of physical grief, but it did set into motion my deceptive capabilities of lying. I was the only one who ate that pie and didn't get sick. John and his brother became violently ill a few hours after ingesting it. Of course, everyone was trying to figure out *what* could have made them both so sick. All possible variables were investigated, and through the process of elimination everyone zeroed in on the chess pie. The only catch was, I too had eaten that pie — and I was fine! Ironically I felt like the cat who had swallowed the mouse when everyone looked to me for a possible explanation. I had none, so I lied!

"I thought about having a piece of that pie, but I decided against it," I quickly replied while looking them squarely in the eye. You see, no one had actually seen me eat a piece. It even may have been the piece I secretly shoveled into my mouth while bending over the kitchen sink to eliminate the evidence of crumbs. No one knew anything for sure; only me, and I knew for sure I must lie. And I did!

In some ways I think it may have been better if I *had* gotten sick. At least then I could have been miserable *with* someone. As it was, I was alone in my misery. My lying drove me further into the secrecy of my misery, and I stood isolated from those around me.

Lying was a choice I made because of my addiction to food. It was a choice I am not proud of, but one I thought necessary to keep my mask in place. I wanted no one to know the truth of my trickery, and, at the time, no one did. Satan is the father of lies (John 8:44), and I had bonded with him through my behavior and deception.

The Joy Robber

Satan is a joy robber. He certainly robbed my joy for years as I continued to make choices centered on food. This was very much apparent when I balked and bucked with John about camping. Camping, to John, meant tenting, and it was supposed to be a fun family activity, but for me it threatened close quarters, no bathrooms, no refrigeration, and a limited food supply. How would I manage under those circumstances? Wouldn't it be easier to stay home? Home was the safety net where I could get away to be alone, go to the bathroom on demand, and get my hands on food when the urge to eat surfaced. Tenting seemed too risky.

Well, the family won, and John bought a tent. How could he say no with two children eager to conquer the wilds in something as primitive as a tent? I grinned and gritted my teeth as we landed at the campground. I wanted to be home and *alone.* Yet everyone else was having a grand time. Why couldn't I join in the fun? What was fun? When would we leave?

My fun was food! It robbed me of my joy with my family. I thought about food every waking moment of my life. It took great energy and manipulation to endure these camping trips, and only in retrospect can I see how food kept me from enjoying my family. I couldn't join in the fun; keeping my secret required me to be vigilant and on the alert for discovery. Food worked well to isolate me, exactly what Satan needed to divide my relationships and to lure me away from those fun times.

I never wanted to admit the power food had in my life. For years I thought I wasn't hurting anyone by my secret. I was deceived into thinking that food did not alter my thought processes like alcohol or drugs, but I realize now that it did. Food was like a drug because it anesthetized my mind and my soul into deadness. As a result, I felt no real joy or sadness. Instead, I ate to retain balance and control.

Food further interrupted my relationships because I lied and cheated to maintain them. At the time it didn't seem like that was what I was doing. It all seemed to come very naturally to me. But now I know deception was my survival tactic.

It is an awful way to live. Only Satan could twist and conjure up such a lifestyle. And only God could unravel and shed light into the darkness this secret had made of my life. I needed to see myself in the light of God's truth, and eventually I did. I needed to believe God, and in due time I did. The chains of bondage needed to be broken, and they were. It was a process—one that took much searching, but one that is possible.

Chapter Six

Counseling: Convicted of Sin

I was notorious for recommending counseling to my friends who had problems. Of course, I had never considered counseling for myself, but I could see its merit for others. In March of 1989 my friend Sandy called to say she had a "great opportunity" for me. The Institute of Biblical Counseling was looking for someone who would be willing to be counseled by one of their interns at no cost. The only catch was the sessions would be videotaped with the possibility of using those tapes as a teaching tool for their upcoming seminars at an institute held for pastors, counselors, lay counselors, students, and other interested people who had previously attended a basic seminar. She was very positive and enthusiastic about this "great opportunity." Would I be willing to be that counselee?

A feeling of dread swept over me. Why did she call? Did she think I had a problem? Why me? Interestingly enough, I was the first person who came to Sandy's mind when she was asked if she knew of anyone. It wasn't so much that I was a mess or had a problem, but more that I was responsible and she knew if I started I would finish. They didn't want anyone who would bail out prematurely; she knew I would deliver. Sandy asked me to pray and think about it.

After I hung up, I told John about her call and request.

"I'm not going to do this. No way will I be counseled, and especially on videotape. I won't be anyone's guinea pig." John was supportive as he replied, "You don't have to do anything you don't want to."

It was settled. I wasn't going to do it. Now all I had to do was call Sandy back. I wondered who was second on her list. I decided to give it a day before calling her; besides, I did say I would pray about it.

As the next day approached, I could not get this counseling out of my mind. I had always said if I were to get counseling it would be from I.B.C. So what was the big deal? It was free. Maybe I could get some answers to those questions surfacing in my mind about my past. I didn't have to say anything I didn't want to. No one could force out all my secrets. I would be in control of what I chose to tell or not. Maybe I could be healed of my eating disorder without ever admitting I had one! It all sounded promising—I would do it.

Counseling but Still Hiding

As my first counseling session loomed ahead of me, my anxiety accelerated. Sandy assured me my counselor, Bob (not his real name), would be good for me. He sounded nice over the phone, but I was really nervous. Was it possible to see my eating disorder? What if he asked anything about food in my life? He was a professional trained to see hidden secrets of the soul. Would he see mine? How could I hide my passion for food from him? This could take more skill than I thought—was I up to the challenge?

Certainly. A big part of that challenge was to make absolutely sure I looked good. That meant well dressed, groomed, and polished right down to my fingertips. I wanted to make a good impression. That was very important; not only for Bob to see, but I wanted to look convincing and presentable on those tapes. With first base covered I could move on to second base.

Food—I ate lunch just before the sessions. No empty,

growling stomach would give me away. I didn't want to draw any unusual attention to the part of my anatomy that required feeding. Keep it full and quiet. Confidently, I moved to third base.

Rehearsal—I had over an hour's drive to each session. This proved to be plenty of time for me to rehearse exactly what I would reveal each time. I toyed with certain topics, confident I could survive their scrutiny. With that settled I was sliding onto home plate.

Relief—I made it through the sessions without my eating disorder being uncovered. So far so good. My strategies were working. This hadn't been so bad after all. Not a word had been mentioned about food. I was home free.

But was I as relieved as I thought? Not really. An unspoken part of my counseling strategy was a deep desire to be understood. I went into each session thinking that if Bob knew all I had been through, all that I had suffered, and all of my pain, he would excuse me for any behavior that might be sinful on my part. Somehow I could be the exception to the rule and require no change. Unfortunately, that is, in part, what I got from Bob.

I didn't realize at the time what was happening. I was so relieved to have someone listen to me. He was very understanding and empathized with me. It felt good, and in my mind justifiable, but it had little effect on the pain in my soul. It wasn't until I stopped seeing Bob that feeling good and justified didn't make me feel *better*. Something was still wrong.

I was responsible for this because I hid my eating disorder from him. But I freely talked about my past sexual abuse. Over the last couple of years I had done enough reading on sexual abuse and eating disorders to make the connection between the two. A friend had mentioned her sexual abuse to me while we stood in my kitchen preparing lunch. Another friend casually mentioned over the phone a memory of abuse similar to my own. God used my reading and my friends to prepare me to look at the abuse. My memories were not hidden; I just never put them together and identified them as abuse. Having an eating disorder compounded the necessity for me to discuss my sexual abuse.

Sexual Abuse

I brought the sexual abuse up in the sessions. It was not as shameful to me as the eating disorder. I could see myself a victim in the abuse, but the eating disorder was all my own choosing. I felt to blame for perpetuating it for so long, and didn't want anyone, including Bob, to know about it. But I was not responsible for Bob circling the abusive issues with me. He thought healing was in affirming me and offering me understanding—something he could not do. Only God could do that for me.

Bob did clarify and validate that abuse had taken place, but he was not willing to open the wound. I felt a measure of compassion from him, but it was not enough. I needed him to walk into the muck with me, to stay in the abuse and my pain.

Appendix B, at the end of this book, is a chart taken from Dan Allender's book *The Wounded Heart* that defines the types of sexual abuse. My contact abuse was classified as the least severe. My abuse was more in verbal, visual, and psychological interaction. Nevertheless it was enough to damage the female soul, and drive me into eating disorders to deaden my longings to be known and loved as a woman. I had a need to numb the pain any way I could. Food proved to be my source of comfort, and vomiting worked to empty me of the ugliness I felt inside from being female.

As a young girl, I experienced touches to my body that cheapened me as a female. I was snickered at when asked if I had a girdle on to hold up my nylons. I felt something was wrong about being a girl. Overhearing fun poked at the bra I was wearing and couldn't fill out shamed me even more. Left unattended and naked in the bathroom at age seven, I was forced to protect my physical body from being penetrated by an older male. I felt cheap and dirty. A stolen peek at my femaleness through my bedroom window was taken and used against me. No longer were my bedroom or bathroom safe. Someone had violated me in both places.

I fell prey to a setup in a trailer where a boy's nakedness was exposed to me, and I was told secrets about sexual encounters that made me feel used and invaded. It didn't take long to realize I wasn't protected or safe as a female.

As a young girl, what did I do with all this? Nothing. I kept silent and told no one. I felt there must be something wrong with me that caused this to happen. This was only reinforced when I remembered I knew there was a naked boy in the trailer and I went in anyway. Had I been a good girl, I wouldn't have gone in. How could I tell anyone about what was happening? It didn't happen all at once, and I couldn't put it together. It was all very confusing to me. I felt obscene. So I kept quiet, endured, and eventually turned to food to comfort my injured soul.

Bob did not want to get into those abuse issues with me. It was definitely freeing to talk about them, and it felt good to hear him say they were wrong, but that was as far as the counseling went. I kept putting my issues on the table, but he refused to pick them up. I had been "missed" again as a woman who had been sexually abused and didn't even know it!

Where was I to go from here? I went back to Sandy. Something was not right. My eating disorder was still out of control, and now that I had opened the lid on the sexual abuse I needed to talk.

Embracing the Little Girl

With Sandy, I had to walk through the wound left open and bleeding from the sexual abuse. There is no way I could have taken that journey alone. God had always been there for me, but I fully believe He provides others to come along side a wounded heart to help mend the soul. Sandy was the one God provided for me.

As we moved into this journey, I had to take a look at the

little girl left damaged by the abuse. Granted, I was a grown woman, but I needed to recapture the little girl. I knew she was lost because I didn't like her. For years I had turned my back on her. This was not evident until I realized I refused to look at pictures of myself hanging in the home where I grew up. Even as I managed just a glance, I didn't know who she was. To look any longer only surfaced disgust. My solution was to avoid looking at her altogether.

As Sandy and I started to embrace that little girl, I felt a flood of tears and hurt begin to stir. The embrace required me to enter her thoughts, emptiness, hurts, and shame. I wasn't sure I could do it. It was too painful to remember and to feel for her. I felt really lost and alone. Sandy entered my pain as she listened to the memories and cried over my loss. Was it really possible the little girl was innocent, good, and enjoyable? Was it possible there was nothing wrong with who I was?

It became very evident that the toughest thing for me to be, was simply what I was—a woman. Growing up as a female did not feel safe. There was something immoral with being a girl. I found myself unsuccessfully trying to be something I was not—a boy.

When I was five years old, I wanted to be one of the guys. I removed my shirt to run bare-chested with them. They shamed and laughed at me. When I attempted to stand up to go to the bathroom I failed and, worse yet, got caught trying by a man. Wasn't this something I had seen a man do in the bathroom? More embarrassment and shame. What was wrong with this little girl?

Nothing was wrong with the little girl. Nothing was wrong with me. I was a woman designed exactly as God intended for me to be. It took many sessions with Sandy and much prayer for me to realize this truth. I can't put my finger on the exact moment this truth took root in my heart, but I do know the change gradually took place.

My mother had been gone for over two years. It was springtime, and I was back home unpacking my father's things from Florida. I took many trips up and down the stairs as I put his clothes away. On one of those trips the little girl caught my eye. She was sitting on a platform, posed nicely in a green corduroy skirt and jacket. Her blouse was pale pink with gold buttons, and one hand rested on her knee while the other supported her from behind. Soft brown curls framed her face, and she was smiling. I had passed that picture hundreds of times over the years, always purposefully avoiding it. Today I stopped and looked. Tears came as I recognized her. She was me! And I was beautiful.

I wanted her to jump out of the picture so I could hold her in my arms and smell the fragrance of her innocence. I longed to look into her eyes and feel her hair. She was truly "pretty as a picture."

It felt good—I felt good! By identifying her, I saw myself and was finally able to embrace and comfort the little girl. She was not lost. God had protected her all those years, and He had returned her to me.

A change had taken place. My wounded heart was mending but not yet fully healed. I had a glimmer of hope even though my eating disorder was still a part of my daily ritual. Did I have the courage to continue the journey? I began to plow ahead.

Could Sin Be a Problem?

My counseling with Sandy took place during the eight months I waited for the videotapes to arrive from I.B.C. Although the Institute had assured me I would be able to view the tapes before the seminar and that the tapes would not be used without my approval, I felt obligated to give my OK. How would I be able to say no after all the time, effort, and expense of so many people? I waited with sweaty anticipation for those tapes to arrive.

Arrive they did, three months before the first advanced seminar was scheduled to take place. I didn't have much time to process these tapes and evaluate my performance. I had to get busy. I was curious to see what the two other counselors who were critiquing the tapes would say.

As I watched the first tape I found myself very critical of everything—my hair, my voice, my gestures, my honesty. I had unloaded everything I could think of—except the bulimia. As I watched, I was looking for any clues that would unlock the bondage of my eating disorder. I read suspicion into every statement Bob and the other two counselors said—I was looking for discovery while being safely hidden.

As I proceeded into the second tape, I was still searching. The answer to my eating disorder had to be in there somewhere. So far I was hearing the word "sin" being mentioned, but could not see any connection with it for myself. I endured some critical remarks about my relational style— nothing new to me, but a little hard to swallow considering they were on videotape. My jaw locked even as I so much wanted to be free. At one point Bob referred to me as a "pill" to live with. Because of his southern accent I totally missed his derogatory remark. In my arrogance I asked him to repeat it. He did! Lovely—now no one else would miss it either.

Well, it all came to a head in the third tape. After I disclosed everything I could think of—except the bulimia—the bottom line was I did not see my sin. How dare anyone say that about me? MY SIN! Whatever could it be? Remember, I was the innocent victim in all of the abuse. Granted, my bulimia was in full force, but these counselors didn't know that!

In my panic to try and figure this tape out, I had Sandy come and view it with me. I was hoping she could enlighten me and soften the unjust blow I had received. We ate lunch while we watched. (How ironic!) We stopped the tape several times to discuss the teaching. Sandy was patient and a measure of comfort, but she didn't tell me my sin. I found out later she didn't know what it was either. What could it be?

I knew it couldn't be my bulimia—that was between God and me. But was it really? Through the teaching on those videotapes, I was finally driven to deal with my sin. My bulimia was still hidden, but my arrogance was very apparent.

In God's Word I discovered what my sin was. Ultimately my sin was my arrogance against God and His finished work on the cross. Psalm 51:4 says, "Against Thee, Thee only, I have sinned." My arrogance cheapened His grace, His forgiveness of my sins, and His love for me. I had chosen food as a counterfeit for God to fill the void of my emptiness. By the time I went to the counseling seminar I had figured that out. Praise God! In His timing He dealt with me and my sin. God used those videotapes to change my life!

The Seminar: A Test of Endurance

The "bulimia battle" was over. It was finished. I could endure attending the seminar knowing the goodness of God had changed me. Endure the seminar is exactly what I did because I was still hiding. After twenty-five years, no one knew the struggle, and no one knew the victory. This time my secret was the work God had done in my life.

I almost lost my cool at that first seminar as rage began to surface. My rage was toward others as they saw my arrogance, the very sin I had confessed to God. I wanted to explain myself but couldn't without revealing my past bulimia. My rage was at myself for being so committed to hiding. I began to wonder if I would ever risk telling the whole story.

I'm thankful for friends who were there with me. Sandy and her husband, Bill, protected the vulnerability that was starting to show as my countenance began to soften. They didn't know the whole story but were willing to be there for me. Sandy was there in her compassion as my life was viewed by all those in attendance, and Bill in his strength as he always made sure I was sandwiched between him and Sandy when the tapes were shown. Both provided the safe place I needed.

The Second Time Around: and Here Comes Shame

Before John and I attended the second seminar, we watched the videotapes—separately. I found it very difficult to sit and watch those tapes alone with him. My arrogance was so obvious on the tapes, and I felt very much ashamed by my haughty behavior. Surely John would see this and prematurely invade my secret. It was better for him to see them alone in case he felt obligated to comment to me about them. I couldn't bear to be seen in my sin—yet! It was enough knowing that having John with me would bring into play a whole new set of dynamics that were not present before.

During this seminar the tough girl reared her head as I tried to be unaffected and in control. Yet John felt my vulnerability and wanted to be strong for me. I didn't want to be needy and protected. I wanted things to be and look normal. Impossible. I was still hiding, and didn't want him or anyone else to get too close.

On top of my hiding, shame reared its twisted head. We were into the second day getting ready to view the second tape. John and I were in a room with approximately sixty other people, waiting for the necessary adjustments for the tape to be shown. I decided to go to the rest room before the tape was to begin and told John, who responded, "OK, your Highness!"

Being called "your Highness" started a flood of emotions. Could John actually think I enjoyed this exposure and being the "star" of the show? Were others thinking that? I immediately felt naked, seen, found out and known in my depraved spirit. I wanted to flee from the presence of all these people, John in particular. Fear reared its ugly head as I started to think that no one here was going to like me. I was sure I was going to be rejected. These feelings of rejection brought to the surface how I really felt about myself as a woman.

By the time I reached the bathroom I was beating myself up for the clothes I had chosen for the day. All of a sudden my black jumpsuit was not feminine and did not seem appropriate—was it too tight? Sexy? Evil? As I glanced at the mirror my makeup didn't look good. My eye shadow wasn't the right color and my lipstick seemed too red. My hair was short—too short for a lady. I felt like a whore!

By now my shame was running full speed ahead. My only defense was to shift the shame from myself onto others. In my mind I began to demand repentance from John for saying that to me. Anger welled up as an unforgiving spirit took over. I began to plot out maneuvers to bring this situation under my control. The silent treatment seemed the best way to handle John. I really wanted to be alone and isolated, but that simply wasn't possible without being noticed by the others. The best I could do was for John and me to move together to the back of the room away from the group. I felt justified! I didn't want to be here in the first place. It was all his fault! Why did I get caught in this situation?

I had gotten my way. As we were moving my friend asked, "What's wrong?" and I lied and abruptly said, "Nothing!" Heaven forbid someone would guess my shame and discomfort. What else could I do but lie and self-protect?

I didn't think I could endure watching that videotape again. The farther back we sat, the less defined my face looked! Good! I didn't want to see myself anyway. Watching myself in pain on the screen, and sitting there in shame, was more than I could endure.

At that moment I did not trust anyone, not even God. I felt everyone in that room had the power to judge me. Even trusting John would ultimately bring me harm. I held contempt for them all. I felt betrayed!

As John and I settled into our seats in the back of the room, I was balled into a tight fist. The lights were dimmed as the tape rolled. That was helpful because I didn't want to be seen. I was stiff as John slid his arm around me and leaned into my shameful world to say he was sorry. I felt invaded by the enemy.

But—there was a certain warmth and familiarity to his touch and genuine remorse in his voice. Was it enough? Probably not, but I had a choice to make. The adversary of my soul had taken me on a trip through shame. Was I going to give him victory and stay there?

I knew in that moment what had happened as I recognized the shame. It was illegitimate! My tight fist would keep me separated from John and ultimately from God. John should not have said what he did, and he knew it, but for me to harbor the shame and use it against him and our relationship would only strengthen that fist. I turned to God and asked Him to forgive me for believing the shameful lies. Only after my repentance was I able to reach up with an unclenched fist to touch John. God had given me the grace to move toward John and to reach out and love him.

Once I did that, it felt good. I realized I needed John and his support. He had made a mistake, and illegitimate shame almost led me to make a bigger one. When I turned it over to God, He took care of my shame. I could stand tall with my shoulders straight as I looked others in the eye. God gave me the strength and the confidence I needed to be a woman of integrity and perfect in His sight.

I looked good! My jumpsuit was fine, my makeup matched, and my hair was short, curly, and feminine. I was a lady, and I would be OK.

This experience was a real turning point. I was able to recognize it for what it was and move on in a direction that was pleasing to God. Since then I have been able to see how shame wants to get a foothold in my life, and I know the choices. I wish I could say I've made the right choice each time, but that has not been the case. Shame has a way of working a slightly different twist each day, and I still have to work on it. The only thing that does not change is God's faithfulness. He is always there to pull me through and extend His grace into my life.

Off the Hot Seat and Coasting

As the week of the seminar moved to a close, John and I were more comfortable with our situation. Little did I know that people were so caught up in their own issues they really weren't looking at mine as closely as I thought. My sin only reemphasized their own. People, on the whole, were very kind and gracious to us. The seminar proved to be a safe place for both John and me.

We were glad to be off the "hot seat," and to get home. During this week it had crossed my mind to tell John about God's work in my life and my past struggle with eating disorders, but it seemed too risky. Was it, or I, too much to handle? I was committed to coasting for a while longer. I knew sooner or later I would be telling John. It could wait.

Chapter Seven

Sexual Abuse: A Struggle for Femininity

For four years I always had a good excuse *not* to attend the Sexual Abuse Support Group that met each week at my church. *That* particular evening was conveniently filled with Jeff's or Jenny's athletic events. Besides, I was no longer practicing my eating disorder, so I wondered if I really needed to attend after all. Sandy and I had hammered out my abuse issues. Wasn't that enough? Couldn't I just avoid this part of my recovery process? However, I knew these were not valid excuses, and finally I attended my first meeting. My eyes scanned the room while my mind quickly registered the count. I tallied who was there, who wasn't there, and who was surprised I was there. Other women seemed to be doing the same. Was I consciously taking roll? Will I be this censorious in heaven?

As a victim of sexual abuse, I felt if I could just air all my abusive issues, I would be able to get on with my life. The struggle would be over, and I would be normal. (I'm still trying to decide: What is normal?) Unfortunately, that was not the case. I have found that sexual abuse has an insidious way of creeping into every part of my womanhood. I did not even realize this for myself, much less for others, until I started to examine the secondary damage of abuse: the defensive ways we develop to deal with our fears and pain. For twelve weeks our group took a closer look at this secondary damage.

It was during these twelve weeks that I realized *more* was required of me. Hadn't I done enough? Evidently not, because God began to untie the restraints knotting the woman inside of me. I wasn't fully aware of this untying process, but I was soon to find out that change was necessary. Change occurs through the avenue of repentance. So once again I was faced with choices: Would I choose my defensive ways based on lies and unbelief? Or would I choose God's way based on truth? Was I willing to unravel the knots of unbelief?

Are We What We Wear?

It was hard enough to come to grips with the abusive memories, but to have someone explore our wardrobes, cosmetics, hair, bedrooms and refrigerators stirred up a lot of agitation and resistance! These tend to be areas we want to control and use to hide who we are. So to really take a look at how we use them against ourselves and others brings on a whole army of opposition.

In the broad picture, women use their wardrobes in many different ways. Some wear layers of clothes to cover their curves and body in general. Many will not wear dresses or skirts because they belong specifically to a female, and this is who they are trying to protect. Many women wear "little girl" style clothing to keep men away. Many choose drab colors to avoid calling attention to themselves, and some simply dress "frumpy." The bottom line is that often a woman uses her clothes to protect her from possible further abuse and to keep her femininity hidden.

An opposite reaction is that of an abused woman who may dress provocatively, feeling that this attention and further abuse is exactly what she deserves. She doesn't want the abuse, but she challenges it by the clothes she wears. A certain hope within her says maybe this time the responses will be different, and it is this hope she will cling to.

I never really gave much thought about the way I dressed having anything to do with my abuse. My wardrobe was fantastic! I dressed to the nines, so to speak. But in looking back I realize I had spent a lot of money and time creating an image for myself. This image was so stylish and good looking, no one could see beyond it. I used to wear hats to match every outfit, even at a time when no one wore hats. My hats intimidated people! They served me well. Between my hats and high fashion I was unapproachable, isolated, and insulated.

In all of this I never wore anything fitted, especially jeans. For me, there was a certain "whorish" look to them, and I did not want anyone, men in particular, to focus on that part of my anatomy.

It wasn't until I joined the support group that I was able to put my sexual abuse and wardrobe together to see how deceived I was. Eventually I didn't need clothes or hats to hide anymore! Repentance for me was to remove the hats and be seen. Renewal was to wear fitted jeans knowing full well I was *not* a whore.

What Do We Make of Makeup?

The cosmetics drawer causes women to squirm as they look at themselves in the mirror. Do they like what they see? Many times not! Some will resort to lots of makeup to cover their face so as not to be seen—or to draw attention to their face to detract from the rest of their body—or to make themselves look like the whore they falsely believe they are.

Some wear no makeup. They choose to go "as they are," not wishing to cover any flaws or enhance their assets. Makeup takes time and skill to apply, and many women feel they simply don't qualify for the effort. They do not want to look any better because on the inside they feel unattractive.

I never thought there was any connection between my makeup and my abuse. I wore makeup just like my clothes: very stylish, neat, and attractive. It never occurred to me that my lipstick caused me anxiety. You see, it was the first item of makeup I experimented with on my first day as a seventh grader. I was on my way out the door, lips painted a soft pink, and feeling very grown up. Lipstick signalled a new beginning as I left grade school behind and crossed over into junior high. I was ready to enter this new class in a new building. I hoped that my lipstick would be noticed, but I was totally unprepared for the snide remarks and laughter that accompanied me through the kitchen.

"What is that red stuff on your face? You are not going to school looking like *that* are you?" I blushed with shame and embarrassment. I couldn't wash that lipstick off fast enough. As my friend Pat and I walked down the driveway, she wanted to know why I wasn't wearing the lipstick she and I had bought and planned on wearing together. I noticed with envy the lipstick freshly displayed on *her* lips.

"I decided against it," was my reply. I was humiliated and disappointed that my attempt at being "grown-up" had failed so badly.

Seems like a trite and insignificant incident, but I've never forgotten it, and it ruled my lips for years. Not only was wearing it a problem, but I've always had trouble getting it on and staying within the confines of my lips. It was either crooked, not finished off, or it would smear. I'm still not sure if my inability to apply lipstick was due to fumbling dexterity or an emotional block. Therefore, even as an adult, I gave up and would not wear it.

It wasn't until I really gave this some thought that I recognized where my abuse affected me. I've always connected lips with high sensuality. As a seventh grader, I remember Doris Day applying red lipstick to full, luscious lips in public places in front of men. It seemed so feminine, yet a "come-on." As a result the feminine side of lipstick was lost to me. I felt like a "come-on" girl as my lips turned into a high-risk physical attraction. They were (and still are) very sensual, and I never wanted men to think I was being seductive with my lips.

Consequently, I had to take a closer look at my lips to see them as a part of my femaleness. A part that was legitimate.

God did not intend my lips to be a threat to me. They were His design, and they were mine! Repentance for me was to wear lipstick, even red, and to apply it as needed wherever I was. It has been good. I haven't seduced anyone with my lips—they are safe, and so am I!

It has been good to get over this hurdle even though remembering has caused me pain. The group process has been instrumental in this remembering, and God has His way of bringing into light what I need to know, when I need to know it.

Soft Curls

Hair is supposed to be a woman's crowning glory, and to some it is, but to a victim it too can seem dangerous and be used to keep others under control. Straight, short, severe cuts are masculine—perfect to ward off men. Cutesy cuts and ponytails are little-girlish—no one will approach their wearer as a woman or require her to be one. Dirty, unkempt hair is disgusting and will keep people at a distance. Bangs can cover the face and long hair, the breasts—perfect for hiding.

My hair has been short, really short, for years. It wasn't until two years ago that I moved into a high-risk coiffure of curls. To me curls were the height of femininity. They were gentle, inviting, and flirtatious—the direct opposite of the straight, off-the-forehead look I had always preferred and that served me well to add a rigid and severe profile to my womanhood. Could I really risk curls? Of course! Curls proved to be a form of repentance as I ventured exposing my vulnerability and began to enjoy curls' softening effect on my countenance, a softening that deserves to be enjoyed by others.

The Struggle with Sex

As the support group moved into the bedroom, things really became difficult. Here a victim is definitely in jeopardy.

Feelings of betrayal surface as we remember how sexuality was used against us. To learn to trust anyone, including our husbands, is very risky. Sex is something we would rather do without or perform as a duty to our mates. For a victim to enter into the pure enjoyment of sex seems whorish and unthinkable.

It is not unusual to find victims wishing they had never married. Many abused women spend a lot of time and mental energy avoiding their husbands and conjuring up ways to put off sexual involvement. They may feel a measure of guilt about this avoidance, but they feel an equal measure of self-justification that prevails and firmly roots the wedge of separation already in existence.

Something totally unexpected happens to some abuse victims after they utter the words "I do." The "I do" becomes "I do not" in the bedroom. What could very well have been sensually exciting prior to marriage becomes repulsive after those words are spoken. Some choose premarital sex and find it physically fulfilling, but add marriage's emotional and psychological involvement, and many victims cannot give all that is required for the bonding and design God had intended.

Because of the fall, we are all going to struggle. But the sexual abuse victim will struggle more because her fear of intimacy and invasion is more intense, especially during recovery. As a victim awakens to her emotions, she begins to realize what she has been missing in a sexual relationship. She discovers a husband who has settled for less than all of who she could be. Both find themselves struggling with God's intended design for man and woman. What may have started out as *her* problem indirectly shifts to *their* problem. Both will need to face the other honestly in their sexuality.

Another area of struggle for an abuse victim is the powerlessness she perceives in having no say over when, where, or how sex will happen. Because she had no control over her sexuality when she was abused, she thinks she must perform sexually each time she is asked, whether she wants to or not. The thought of saying no never occurs to her because it was not an option for her during the abuse. It is quite a revelation for a victim to recognize that she has a choice and can exercise that choice.

Food and the Unforgettable Five

The last area of damage I would like to address is found in our refrigerators. Food is a big issue for abuse victims as we take a look at how we use it in our lives. Food anesthetizes our senses of thinking and feeling. Why suffer the agony when we can eat? Food not only dulls the senses, it keeps the memories of abuse locked inside as we continually stuff them down. Food can soothe away hurts and be a companion—it requires nothing from us in return. It can be controlled. Food is so available and acceptable.

Unfortunately, we use food as a camouflage. As victims get heavy, they enjoy the insulation their weight provides for their bodies. It hides the feminine curves and turns men away. To lose weight and regain curves is just too scary—better to stay fat and unattractive. Food keeps us from intimate relationships. It is safer to be isolated than risk possible rejection.

When these issues are brought to a victim's attention, she often responds with open hostility. Many women are touchy about their weight and don't like to think that something as necessary and benign as food could be so destructive. They covet their favorite foods and get angry when someone suggests change. Food brings out the depraved nature in some women who resort to stealing it, hiding it, hoarding it, and sneaking it. I can assure you that no one likes to have this revealed!

I know firsthand the damage caused by food. Food was my life, my occupation, my friend. I didn't need people; I had food! I was trapped in this addictive cycle and had given up hope of ever getting out. It wasn't until I looked at the sexual abuse that I began to see the dangerous role food was playing. I still felt trapped, but clarifying the abuse opened the door for me to see my sin and find my way out of this addictive behavior.

Repentance for me required that I *turn from food to God*. I had to confess my arrogance in thinking I could control my life with food. I had made food my god when the reality was that I needed to *believe* God! When I asked God to take over and fill the emptiness I was filling with food, He proved more than sufficient for my need!

I've thought much on this topic over the years. I've been asked, "Have you eaten five chicken legs since your recovery?" Good question! I really hadn't given *that* particular perspective much thought. Could I eat those five chicken legs as a recovered food addict, knowing full well they were part of the catalyst sending me on the downward spiral of addiction? The only way to find out was to try it. I did! And, I found I could indeed eat five chicken legs without guilt, remorse, or the urge to purge.

Were eating those chicken legs a form of repentance? I believe so. It doesn't mean I'll have to eat five every time, but I was able to give up my deceptive thinking and see there was nothing wrong with eating them. I lived through it. Why? Because God's way—facing painful truth—always brings life.

Victims Are Survivors!

Opening the wound of sexual abuse was a necessary part in my total recovery. God had a unique way of taking me where I needed to go to see His grace in all of this.

I wish women did not have to suffer the pain of sexual abuse. I wish I hadn't. People need to understand that the damage to the soul goes deep as victims struggle to survive such abuse. We are survivors! If not for God's grace, many of us would have been dead by now. It is just so hard for us to see how sexual abuse creeps into all areas of our feminine soul. It is not enough to deal with the abuse; *we have to deal with our entire femininity*.

I trust that what I have written will enlighten those interested in ministering to the sexually abused. I trust, too, that you will be patient as women plow up this area of their lives left dormant for years. Be ready to rejoice as victims slowly recover their womanhood. Recovery is a process, and with God's guidance recovery is possible.

What Is Repentance?

Repentance is the vehicle necessary for change to occur in a victim's life. *Change does not come from remembering, forgiving, talking about it, or being a member of a support group*, although these may contribute to change. True repentance that brings about change comes *when we turn from living our way to living God's way*. Repentance is not neutral. We must give up our defensive ways of living. Repentance comes moment by moment, and is different for everyone. It is not a one-time thing, and it changes.

Sometimes repentance is so subtle that it is not noticed by many people. It can be quiet, lonely, and private. Likewise it can be very dramatic and even embarrassing. Why? Because, at first, it often feels uncomfortable, but gradually it feels wonderfully freeing. Repentance is a cause for celebration in anyone's life, including my own.

What would repentance be for me today? Possibly to slip on a hat again! Would I still be open and inviting? Maybe I'll just have to wear one and see. . . .

Chapter Eight

Recovery:
A Place of Repentance

Recovery from my eating disorder proved to be a process. It started when I received Christ as my personal Savior, but most of the intensive work has taken place during the last five years. It was a painful journey through my past and into my soul. It was a journey I was reluctant to take and was sure would only lead me back to the binging and purging I was so familiar with. It was not a journey I set upon with confidence, but more one of sheer desperation to put a stop to this loathsome behavior. I had no idea what paths my journey would take; I only knew I must begin.

God was gracious as He led me on this journey. He brought people, circumstances, and situations at just the right time. I was not even aware He was leading, and I was not a conscious follower. All I knew was that I was sick and tired of eating and vomiting. It had to stop—I was exhausted. I was forty years old—too old to be struggling with this. Visions of being a grandmother hanging my head over a toilet vomiting my insides out haunted me.

Longing to Be Known

My mother's death in 1987 brought to the surface my own mortality. She died at age seventy-five. That was thirty-five years down the road for me. Would I eat and vomit my way to age seventy-five?

My mother's death awakened in me a loneliness I had never felt before. Even food could not deaden the aloneness that gripped my soul as I mourned the loss of someone so close to me. I never wanted my mother to discover the shame of my eating disorder; now I knew she never would. She had left me, and I had escaped her scrutiny into my soul.

Loneliness followed me like a shadow wherever I went. Food did not even taste good, but it served to fill the empty place my mother had left. It was not satisfying, but it was familiar. My vomiting only left me longing for more—but more of what?

It has been my experience that what I long for never comes to the surface without tears. My mother's death brought tears to my soul. In the past I had guarded my tears carefully. I was not familiar with "happy" tears, only tears that released pain for short intervals before I drew them back inside. They always signaled something was wrong.

But these tears for my mother signaled my longing to be known as a woman. I realized my mother hadn't known me, and now it was too late. John was the next closest person to me, and he and my children really didn't know me either. I had used food to numb the longing in my soul to be known because I believed that who I was would not be acceptable or good enough. For me to be known, I would have to allow myself to be truthful, seen, discovered, discerned, recognized, and involved in an intimacy that could be perceived as sexual—all very risky because I had used food to hide myself as a woman. Could I ever risk the discovery of being known?

I started to realize that if I were to die, no one, not even my husband or children, could say they really knew who I was.

I used to wonder, *What would my children say about me if I were to die? Would they refer to me as warm, nurturing, soft, honest, enjoyable, understanding, loyal, and lov-*

able? Frankly, I don't think so! They more likely would have said, "She cooked, cleaned, did laundry, shopped, and attended all our activities in a supportive manner." My role was no different than a hired maid. As much as I wanted to be known as a woman, I just could not see my way clear to the vulnerability it required. Food's numbing effects took control over relationships.

So the mask remained securely in place for a few more years. But God was wooing me to Himself by giving me a desire to become alive. At the very least I knew there could be something different for me in being known. I had no idea this would be a part of my recovery, but God knew where He was leading me and how long it would take. The journey was underway.

Continuing the Journey

The second stage of my journey to recovery started when Sandy and I opened the wounds of sexual abuse. Not all women with an eating disorder have been sexually abused but, according to Pam Vredevelt in *The Thin Disguise* (NavPress, 1990), eating disorders usually start with a trauma, often a form of sexual abuse (page 157). Dan Allender in *The Wounded Heart* confirms that many bulimic women have a history of sexual abuse (page 150). I know of only one woman who can, without a doubt, say her eating disorder was not due to sexual abuse. It is not my intention to say that every woman with bulimia has been sexually abused, but I do feel it warrants investigation.

Reading about bulimia's connection with sexual abuse enabled me to open the wound of abuse. This process didn't start until I was forty years old, and I had already been in the eating disorder over twenty-three years. I simply could not ignore the obvious any longer.

When sexual abuse surfaced in my counseling with Bob, I felt crushed under the shame of abuse *and* my hidden eating disorder. Later that same day I called Sandy and we wept over the discovery of my abuse. Looking at the abuse was one of the hardest steps I had to take on this road to recovery. But it was definitely a step in the right direction. I didn't even have all the memories of my abuse to draw upon, but I had enough to validate its existence.

God knew all along I was a victim. He mercifully allowed me to feel the hurt and shame while He held me close to Himself. Realizing my victimization was a humbling experience. God provided Sandy at a time when I desperately needed someone to hold onto as we waded through the sexual abuse. But ultimately only God could lead me through and out of the muck abuse had made of my life. God was definitely leading on this journey to recovery.

Many women get stuck in their victimization. It seems a safe and justifiable place to take up residence. The only thing is you'll reside alone because no one can enter into your self-justification! I know because I justified myself to the exclusion of all other intimate relationships for years. As long as I could keep my self-justification in place no one could require me to move into their world as a woman designed to be known, understood, and loved.

Sounds like a pretty tall order for a victim. It was for me. But God was breaking down the justifiable barriers that food had held in place by awakening those longings in my soul. I simply could not deny their existence.

It might seem that having my longing to be known aroused, combined with uncovering and working through the sexual abuse, would be sufficient to unlock the bondage food had on my soul, but they weren't. Both were part of the journey, but I definitely had not arrived. Where could I possibly go next?

Adjust and Self-correct

In my frustration and unwillingness to dig deeper, I took a slight detour on my journey and tried behavioral changes. Forcing myself with sheer willpower, I set out to make the necessary adjustments. Most detours take you off course and work well enough for a while. But eventually you must get back on the main road to arrive at your final destination. So it was with my behavioral changes.

First I tried to eat a normal breakfast—no excessive food so I wouldn't be tempted to vomit. I was able to do that successfully, and I could retain it until lunch. Unfortunately, lunch would explode into the toilet! But after a year of holding down breakfast, I stretched my willpower to get through lunch. It worked, but sadly I could only bite the bullet until 3 P.M. before I would begin my explosion into the toilet. No amount of willpower could get me past 3 P.M. Dinner was never a meal I could eat without vomiting afterward. The behavioral changes went just so far; they were not sufficient to complete the job.

I have to admit that I felt a measure of satisfaction to be able to maneuver my eating for two meals. A sense of normalcy lulled my senses briefly each day. But things deteriorated so fast after 3 P.M. that I was jarred into recognizing the messy reality of my life. My willpower had run its course because I simply could not make any other behavioral changes to completely control my bulimia.

It wasn't until I recovered from my eating disorder that I discovered why behavioral changes weren't enough for a total recovery. Behavioral changes dealt with my outward actions, but they could not appease my inward and emotional turmoil. It is like trying to put out a forest fire with a garden hose. It extinguishes a few flames, but it is not enough to drown the fire. The fuel is stronger than the behavior, causing the fire to burn out of control. The fire of my eating disorder burned on for a few more years until God revealed to me the fuel feeding the flames.

Looking for Love

My soul was coming alive as I continued on my journey and recognized my longing to love and be loved. So far I had carried on a love affair with food. It was an affair that never satisfied, left me longing for more, never fulfilled me as a woman, and left me empty except for shame. I could never fully give myself to someone; likewise I could never fully receive someone. Food always blocked the path to receiving love and reaching out to love others. I didn't think I had any love to give and I didn't feel worthy of receiving any.

Once again God used circumstances and people to bring this longing to the surface. Our son, Jeff, had graduated from high school and was looking forward to college with excitement, anticipating freedom and new experiences. He couldn't wait to go. I could only watch with dread, wondering how he had arrived at this time in life so quickly. Had I, his mother, equipped him to leave? I knew after he left things would never be the same when he returned. What had I given of myself to Jeff? What of himself had he left me?

After Jeff was gone, I felt alone and empty. The same feelings of loss swept over me as when my mother had died. The only difference was that Jeff was still alive. I really loved Jeff. Did he know that? I longed for him to know that my love went beyond all that had been provided for him. Up until this point, provision was what seemed most necessary. Now all of a sudden I wanted my love to be a warm place in a world that can be cold. I wanted my love to nurture—was it too late?

I was beginning to see that loving Jeff was painful because I wasn't capable of giving all the love Jeff would require. My love was imperfect at best. Loving Jeff would require me to feel disappointment, hurt, loss, inadequacy, and loneliness—all the feelings food had helped me keep under wraps for years. Why now wasn't food working to keep my longings hidden? What was happening inside of me that food could not keep quiet?

Something was stirring within my soul. I wanted more than food to fill my emptiness. It wasn't too late to give my love to Jeff or to anyone else, but could I risk what they might give or not give in return? Would rejection only reinforce my unworthiness? Or would being embraced as a woman feel illegitimate? Could I handle love?

I wanted the answers to these questions, but something was still blocking me. My longings were surfacing, food had lost its numbing effects, I couldn't make any more adjustments to stop binging and purging. My sexual abuse had been clarified and validated; what more could possibly be required of me? I felt very confused and angry. My insides were a jumbled mess as I tried to sort out these new feelings. I even felt betrayed by food because it no longer worked as my protector and friend. I was feeling very vulnerable, exposed, and needy. It did not feel familiar or good!

Out-maneuvering Sin

" 'For My thoughts are not your thoughts, neither are your ways My ways,' declares the LORD. 'For as the heavens are higher than earth, so are My ways higher than your ways, and My thoughts higher than your thoughts' " (Isaiah 55:8-9). Thank goodness! I had lived forty-three years unsuccessfully trying to figure myself out and doing things my own way. During this entire time I never turned to God with my eating disorder! Oh, I confessed the sin of my behavior many times daily, but I never invited Him to enter the pain of my soul keeping me in bondage. My arrogance said, "God, I will take care of this myself. Just forgive my repulsive behavior, *but stay out of my soul.*" My arrogance hated to think I needed God. *My arrogance kept me in unbelief!*

What a position to be in! It is no wonder I felt myself to be a "dangerous" woman with the power I thought I had over God and others. I was truly deceived, not only about myself, but about who God is. Only when I saw the magnitude of my sin, did I realize the generosity of His grace.

Arriving at this point on my journey was part of the process that unfolded as I watched my videotapes. I marvel, not only at God's grace, but at the grace extended to me by the counselors critiquing those tapes. They were truly gentle and kind. The counselors and tapes were all part of the process God used to bring me to Himself and to halt a woman missing the goodness of God in her life.

I wish I could say this was all crystal clear the first time I viewed the tapes. Better yet I wish I had "got it" during the counseling sessions when I was referred to as arrogant. But I didn't! Eight months were to pass before God dealt with my arrogance, but as always His timing was perfect. It was during those eight months that Sandy and I looked at the sexual abuse, a very necessary and painful part of the process. God knew I needed to do that before I could face the deeper work He wanted to do in my life.

Asking for Forgiveness

As a Christian I thought I had a pretty good handle on sin. I knew "right" from "wrong" and was faithfully confessing the "wrongs" on a daily basis. Because I came to the Lord later in life, I could compare the "old" self with the "new" self. I was familiar with 2 Corinthians 5:17, "Therefore if any man is in Christ, he is a new creature; the old things passed away; behold, new things have come." Christ had definitely dealt with the foul-mouthed, drinking woman who passed her days watching soap operas and reading romance novels, but what about the woman with the eating disorder? She was alive and fully conscious of her despicable behavior. How come that didn't pass away along with the other behaviors displeasing to God?

The first answer that comes to mind is that I never asked God to enter my eating disorder and take it away. It was a part of my life I was bent on controlling. *No one* was allowed to enter my banquets and certainly not my vomiting. I asked for forgiveness of sins based on behavior.

My eating disorder was a perfect example of "behavioral" confession. All I ever asked was for God to forgive my eating and vomiting—over and over again. It was tiresome to repeat the same confession numerous times throughout the day, but it became a ritual as sacred as the disorder. It also became mindless repetition. So it went for fifteen years.

Did it ever occur to me to release my eating disorder to God? I believe so, but I quickly snatched it back before I was faced with the dreaded possibility that He could take it from me. What would I do if I couldn't eat and vomit to keep my emotions subdued? I loved and hated the behavior. I loved the numbing effects of food, yet I hated the violence of vomiting. How could I ever turn this over to God? Surely I must get a grip on myself first. This behavior had to be a sin!

And I believed it was. That is why I continued to confess it daily. But the sin of the behavior was not enough to stop me. Even as I believed God's word that says the body is "the temple of God and is holy" (1 Corinthians 3:17), it was not enough. God was really extending me grace here because I rationalized my physical well-being as my reasoning to assume I was not really damaging His "temple." But at the same time I couldn't let God into my "temple" because I knew it was too messy for Him. So I kept Him out!

Even as I write this I am amazed at the sheer arrogance of my thinking. Not only was I slamming the door on God, I was playing roulette with the body He had entrusted to me. I was bent on my own way apart from Him: playing the prodigal, yet longing for more of Him.

Missing God and Life

My excuses had run out. All my resources had dried up. There was nothing else I could do to make my life work. *I had come to the end of myself.* There was no place for me to go but to God, and He was there for me, right where He had always been.

I was weak as I turned to God. I didn't know what to do, where to go, or how to pray. The Holy Spirit ministered on my behalf. "And in the same way the Spirit also helps our weakness; for we do not know how to pray as we should, but the Spirit Himself intercedes for us with groanings too deep for words" (Romans 8:26). The Spirit of God drew me to Himself, and the Spirit began convicting me of sin.

I started to feel guilty. It was not the same guilt I had felt and denied over perpetuating an eating disorder, but a guilt over living as a hypocrite, a justified victim, a liar, and a cheat. For the first time I realized that all I had been through paled in the light of all who God is. God had so much more to offer in my life. I was missing God; I was missing the abundant life only He could give.

Like the children of Israel, I stayed in the wilderness, afraid to enter the land of Canaan because of the giants and unbelief. I, too, feared the giants. My giants were people who seemed to have power over me as a woman. I didn't believe God was my protector who went before me to pave the road of my life. Consequently I settled for glimpses of the abundant life, not realizing I could enter into the whole picture to rest with Him (Hebrews 3).

I was missing the heart of God toward me. "Behold, the Lord God will come with might, with His arm ruling for Him. Behold, His reward is with Him, and His recompense before Him. Like a shepherd He will tend His flock, in His arm He will gather the lambs, and carry them in His bosom; He will gently lead the nursing ewes" (Isaiah 40:10-11). God had promised to be with me, to lead and rule His kingdom, to reward me, exercise justice, and be a shepherd in my life. I was missing Him! Why?

Like a sheep, I had gone astray, seeking my own way (Isaiah 53:6). Anyone seeking her own way apart from God is nothing short of arrogant. My arrogance had kept God away and froze me in unbelief. My arrogance was sin because it denied the blood of Christ on the cross. It said, "Christ didn't die for my eating disorder. God's grace isn't good enough and doesn't extend far enough for my eating disorder. God will forgive everything else in life, except my eating disorder." My arrogance had made food an idol. It kept me from seeking Him. I was my own worst enemy!

It was in God's Word that I began to see the error of my arrogance. Could arrogance be the fuel that kept the fire raging in my soul all these years? Was arrogance fueling the behavioral changes? Is that why they didn't completely work?

In Jeremiah 2:13, the answers to my questions came into focus. "For my people have committed two evils: They have

forsaken Me, the fountain of living waters, to hew for themselves cisterns, broken cisterns, that can hold no water."
Yes, I had forsaken God in this area of my life. Food was my
cistern, idolized for twenty-five years. It was a cracked cistern so I was never filled. Food left me living on empty,
yearning for more, and never satisfied. It was a choice I had
made away from God. A choice I so arrogantly thought I
could manage. My choice proved to be sin!

The Mask Comes Off

There was only one place to go with sin—God! To come
before God I needed to remove the mask and be seen in my
nakedness. There could be no more hiding. It was very
scary to take off the mask and confess my sin. Yet I knew
that with sin there is forgiveness—with forgiveness there is
hope. It was very humbling to come before God, asking
forgiveness for the arrogance that kept me in unbelief. Yet
before I could seek His forgiveness I had to believe not only
the heart of God, but *what God said about me.*

I read and reread Psalm 139. Through this psalm God
gave me a picture of the intimacy He has in penetrating the
human soul. He had searched me, and my sexuality was
known by Him. Even in my hiding He was "intimately acquainted with all my ways." God was present when I was
formed in my mother's womb. He had engineered it all, and
He has always known what is good for me. It was important
for me to believe, "I am fearfully and wonderfully made;
wonderful are Thy works, and my soul knows it very well."
Up until this time my soul did not know it very well. But
God had given me a taste of Himself. He tasted good! God
proved to be safe, trustworthy, and faithful as I removed my
mask before Him.

The Road to Repentance

God was closing in. I came face to face before Him with my
sin, knowing nothing would ever be right until I did. Seeing

my sin and repentance was the turning point on this journey. There was simply nowhere else to go. God had searched my heart and revealed Himself to me. And I believed God! As a result, something had to be done.

I did that something in my car on the way home from the beauty parlor one morning. I was alone, pondering my sin, what I had come to know about God, and what I knew He felt for me. Was I ready to let go and believe truth? Yes, I was!

As I drove through traffic, I began to pray, and for the first time in my fifteen years as a Christian, I asked God to take control of my eating disorder. Through prayer I thanked God for convicting me of my sin. I asked Him to forgive my arrogance in shutting Him out, and I thanked Him for revealing Himself to me. I was perfect and wonderfully made as the woman He created, and I believed it! Because of who He was, I no longer had to be a slave to food. He loved me just as I was. With confidence I was able to say I was finished because *I had believed God.* Only God could fill my spirit with the love and strength required to reach out and embrace others. *When I gave up, God took over.*

My bondage to food had been broken. Actually, that was the easiest part. Living a life open, vulnerable, and continually trusting God was the challenge. Was I up to the challenge? Yes! There really was no other choice for me. If I believed God, I had to live differently. All I had to do was remember those twenty-five years to know I didn't want to go back. God had led me out and I had entered His rest to be His woman. I had repented and chosen God's way. God honors repentance—He honored mine!

Chapter Nine

Sharing the Secret

After I realized that my healing came through filling my emptiness with Christ instead of food, I thought I was finished with this whole process of eating disorders. I just wanted to get on with life and put the pain of those twenty-five years behind me. No one knew of my eating disorder, and I felt no one needed to know. The eating disorder and healing would be my secret, and I could have my own celebration of God's goodness to me without telling anyone else. I felt excited about my healing, but I continued to feel the shame of perpetuating this disorder for so long. I still wanted to hide and keep it a secret.

Now I know that keeping the secret was not a part of God's plan for me. As long as I kept the secret locked inside, I was still living in bondage to the enemy of my soul. For a while this bondage felt safe and in some ways comfortable, but as time went on God brought situations and people into my life that made the hiding more and more difficult.

One of these people walked right through my front door. Her name was Tara. She was staying in our home for the weekend along with several other students from my son's university. Tara arrived late in the evening with two of her friends. I was tired, but committed to stay up and go the

distance with these young and energetic kids if they wanted
to talk. The conversation eventually got around to the one
question I am always asked: "What do you do with all your
time if you don't work?" I was able to share with them
about Bible study at my church, Jenny's sporting events,
and the sexual abuse support group I was involved in. At
this point Tara began to tell of her sister's sexual abuse. I
couldn't help but wonder about Tara's own issues as she so
intensely told about her sister's. I wanted to ask, but didn't
because other people were talking in the kitchen with us.

It was not until the next day when Tara and I were alone
that she told me about *her* abuse and eating disorder. I was
not surprised. She poured out her shame as I listened and
identified with her experience. I shared with her about my
abuse, but I did not tell her about my past struggle with
eating disorders. I wanted to! It was right on the tip of my
tongue, but I held back to protect myself and my secret.

Tara didn't want her friends to know about her eating
disorder (I could readily identify with that), yet she easily
opened up that area of her life to me. At the time I wondered why. Why did God bring Tara into my home? Was this
a coincidence?

It took me a while to see that it was not enough just to be
open before God. He knew all about my problems. He was
present each time I stuffed myself, and likewise He was in
the bathroom each time I vomited. Nothing was hidden
from Him! I had trusted God, but I was not trusting others.
As long as I continued to hide, I would not be free to be the
woman God intended me to be before Him, my husband,
my children, and friends. Could I really trust Him even with
the responses of others? Wouldn't it be safer just to hide?
Was it worth the risk?

War was raging as I struggled with these questions. So
many times I just wanted to blurt it out to whomever was
listening but instead kept the lid on. I was sure that if
anyone knew my secret they would be repulsed by my very
presence. I was equally sure that if John knew, he would
certainly leave me for deceiving him all these years. And my

children would never understand. As long as I dwelt on these lies, my secret was safe. And dwell on them is what I chose to do for a while longer.

Shortly after Tara's visit, I had the opportunity to fellowship with some friends on a retreat. A good friend arrived loaded with food, mainly snacks and sweets, even though all the food had been provided by another committee. She said she felt very threatened and insecure with someone else in charge of *all* the food. She could not trust someone else, and wanted to make sure that food would be available to her. So she brought her own to share.

I really had mixed feelings as I observed my friend and her behavior. A party was going on inside of me as I rejoiced over the fact that I was now free from being so consumed with food that I no longer had to take it with me everywhere I went. I was relieved that I wasn't on the food committee, but was simply free to attend the retreat. I thought back on how many times I had been just like her in having to be in control of all the food brought and served. The thought of not having food immediately available had been paralyzing to me. How different I felt today as I anticipated with surprise what someone else had prepared, and knew that I would enjoy it no matter what it was or when it was served.

But again a battle was brewing as I sat there. I wanted so much to say how well I knew her anxiety and need to be in control of food. How obvious her struggle was to me. My feelings bounced from one extreme to another; from sadness over her preoccupation with food, to delight over my own freedom from the compulsive addiction to food. Yet I said nothing, certain that these women would never understand or trust me again if I told my secret.

The following Sunday, my friend seated herself next to me in Sunday School. I asked her how the rest of the retreat went for her. She looked me square in the eye and said, "Food was a big issue for me this weekend. I just have to have it with me at all times. I need to have something in my mouth. I just don't understand what is wrong with me." I was dumbfounded! Of all the things she could have told me about, she picked food. I immediately went into my self-protection mode for fear she would either guess my secret or I would spill it out right there in class.

The rest of the class was a blur. I could not concentrate on anything except my friend's comment and my intense vulnerability. She had been so honest with me, and yet I continued to hide. How much longer could I keep up this deception?

The conflict continued! Inside I knew that God could use my life with its struggles, but did I really want to be used in all this shameful ugliness? Would people listen and hear Christ's healing in all of this? Or would they get caught up in the abuse and the pure mechanics of what bulimia and vomiting involved? Would I be able to answer graciously the questions people were bound to ask as I unfolded my experience? Could I handle it?

Fortunately, God showed me that I did not have to handle it. He would! On my own I would never be able to expose myself to others, but with Christ I could. I realized that He accepted me in my struggle and continued to love me in the midst of it. He was the One who led me out, and He was the One who would carry me through. To be totally free I knew I had to tell others the secret and rely on God for their responses.

At this point I had been free from my eating disorder for over a year, but I still had told no one. I was anxious and angry, anticipating what had to be done. My anger was a cushion of self-protection as I prepared for the responses of those I would choose to tell. It would hide my vulnerability and keep me safe just in case God couldn't handle it.

It was very enlightening for me to tell other people about my eating disorder and to hear firsthand what they considered to be "the worst" thing I could tell them about myself. For twenty-five years I kept my secret, thinking that people would be totally shocked by my revelation. How surprised I was to find how four very significant people reacted, and what each one anticipated my "secret" would be.

No More Hiding from John

My husband, John, was the first. He was not necessarily the one I would have chosen to be first, but I felt I owed it to him. Telling someone else before him seemed borderline betrayal, even though at the time running it by another friend seemed safer. Nonetheless, John was the first.

There was no easy way to break this news. No rehearsal. I just did it! I was a mess, and had been for days. It was time to let the chips fall where they may.

I sat him down in our kitchen early one morning. He was patient and seemed calmly braced as I announced I had something terrible to tell him about myself. I said it was the worst possible thing! I didn't realize that John's mind was in a whirl as several possibilities surfaced. I launched into my secret, telling him simply that I started out anorexic at age seventeen, moved into bulimia and vomiting at eighteen, and continued in that addictive cycle for the next twenty-four years.

By this time I was sobbing, feeling very shamed and exposed. Now he knew! There was no taking back those words. In between sobs I told him about the sexual abuse. John already knew about that, but I needed to go over it again as my excuse. I continued to talk and justify my behavior. I was afraid to stop and hear what John might have to say.

When I had run out of explanations, John asked, "Is that all?"

"ALL!" I couldn't believe it. What more could there be? I had just told the closest person to me my worst secret, risked exposure and rejection, revealed my total deception in our relationship, and he responded, "Is that all?" In defense I asked, "What did you expect?"

He gave me the answer when I finally stopped my own defense. I found out what was whirling around in his mind. To John the worst possible thing I could tell him was that I had had an affair. Of all things! That was the furthest thing from my mind!

I assured John that my love affair had been with food, not another man. He never realized his biggest competition for my affection was in the refrigerator! In sizing all this up, he was relieved.

John is a man of integrity. He did not want to minimize my past struggle with eating disorders, but in looking at all the options for the "worst" possible thing, he was able to help me put this in perspective.

Now that my secret was out in the open, John could better understand my constant simmering anger and control issues, and we could finally talk about them. What a relief! No more hiding and making excuses! I was surprised to see John's regret at having "missed" me all those years. He was saddened by my loneliness and fear. I did not expect that! Food had done such a good job of numbing my feelings that I had not allowed myself to feel "missed."

I had gotten over the first hurdle by telling someone about my eating disorder. I was no longer alone in my secret. John knew. No more hiding from him. I had trusted God with John's response, and He had taken care of us. Now I was challenged for a lifetime to live with a man who knew all my ugliness. Was God up to this challenge? I am finding the answers to that daily as John and I continue to live, and many times struggle, with our own issues as we try to be honest and open with one another.

Sandy's Relief

It was about three weeks before I mustered up enough courage to tell the next person. By now I had a list of three people I would tell in no particular order. These people were significant, and I wanted to tell them my secret directly. After these three, it really would not matter who found out and when.

Sandy was the next person. She had been counseling me for several months, and she was the one who had arranged the videotaped counseling. She was the first person to validate my sexual abuse, and was the one who walked me through the wound it had created in my soul. Many times in those counseling sessions I wanted to tell her about my eating disorder, but just couldn't. I was too ashamed!

Sandy had known me a long time. She had eaten with me on numerous occasions, commenting on the large amounts of food I could eat and still stay so slim. Yet she never invaded the privacy of my secret to shame me more. In looking back, I'm not sure what I would have done if she had! I think this is why I continued to counsel with her. She was safe and never forced her way into my secrets.

Sandy seemed as relieved as I was that my worst secret was out. Her relief was in part that she, like John, had thought my secret to be something else. What else? I was curious! Sandy thought I had given birth to an out-of-wedlock baby and had given it up for adoption! How interesting!

Jenny Sees My Heart

My daughter, Jenny, was the third person I told. Three weeks after I talked to Sandy, we were vacationing as a family at Maranatha Bible Conference. Sandy had encouraged me to tell Jenny as soon as possible because it was bothering me, but I still found myself holding back.

Jenny was seventeen years old, the only person who had ever questioned me about my eating disorder, and I had lied to her. Telling her involved more than just stating the facts; I had to ask her forgiveness for lying. What if she did not receive me as I told the truth? It was a risk I had to take—the sooner the better.

We were on the beach of Lake Michigan one evening. It was dark, with only the reflection of the moon coming off the water to shed any light. Jenny had been very talkative and open with me and seemed to want to continue our time together. I knew it was the perfect opportunity to tell her because we were alone and the atmosphere was peaceful. A part of me didn't want to ruin this setting with my ugly confession, but I knew that putting it off would not be wise.

I started by telling her I had a secret part of my life she deserved to know about and that it was bad. As I unfolded those twenty-five years, I asked her forgiveness for lying. It was very hard for me to admit that I had stooped to lying to protect myself. I said I was sorry for clouding her judgment and invalidating what she knew the truth to be. I did not make up excuses for myself—I had none and she knew it.

In the darkness of that night, I don't believe Jenny could even see my face, but for the first time she saw my heart. She was able to receive the truth hidden there even as she became angry with me for living the lies. A part of me had not expected this anger from Jenny. I thought she would have been more inclined to pardon me to cover her own vulnerability, but she didn't. She did not offer cheap forgiveness, and I'm glad! She had been put on hold long enough—it was time for her to be angry with me for allowing uncontrollable circumstances in my life to betray her.

Jenny and I worked through the fallout from that night, and we are still working on it. Jenny has forgiven me, and I have been open and honest with her. I now know that had she been quick to excuse me, she would only have been delaying her anger. I'm really thankful she did not do that!

Truth can hurt, but not as bad as lies. Jenny gave me an example of this when she told me she knew all along I was lying to her. If I had admitted to her that I had been vomiting when she asked, she would have accepted that and probably taken it no further, because she did not understand eating disorders. But because I lied, she really was confused and worried. Little did I know that the truth would have protected me more than the lies.

After the air had somewhat cleared that night, I learned just what Jenny had thought my secret was going to be. She had anticipated that I was going to tell her that sometime in my past I had had an abortion. From her perspective as a young Christian woman, that was the worst possible scenario.

Once again I was somewhat surprised. So far sexual immorality was the big secret people thought I was keeping.

I had just one more person to tell, and I started to wonder what my twenty-year-old son Jeff would think when I told him.

Jeff Embraces My Soul

The opportunity to tell Jeff did not present itself for two months. He was on staff at Maranatha Bible Conference for the summer, and it seemed impossible to get him alone. I thought of making an appointment with him, but that seemed too calculated. Somehow I just wanted it to flow naturally into one of our conversations. Well, that never happened!

I don't know why I wanted to protect Jeff from the truth. I had this lofty notion that he thought I was perfect because I was his mother. After all, wasn't I the female role model he would use for his future mate? How could I tell him about my failures?

I was soon to find out that I had underestimated Jeff's ability to handle the truth—and his mother!

In late August Jeff and I were alone in his car on his way back to college. John was following us in our van loaded with Jeff's things. I was at odds as to whom I should ride with that day, but John encouraged me to ride with Jeff. It immediately occurred to me that this would be my perfect opportunity to tell him, but then guilt started to well up as I thought, "What a thing to dump on a kid on his way back to school." I held off for a while, but I knew this was my last chance to be alone with him before I assumed leadership in my Sexual Abuse Support Group in the fall. My eating disorder would definitely come out of the closet there, and I wanted to make sure that he knew first.

Could I write him a letter? I was really struggling with this!

I cried when I told Jeff; I felt I had risked something more than exposure. There was a part of him already lost as a son who had left the nest. I wondered if I would lose even more of him. It was really important that he understand what I had told him because I wouldn't be around on a daily basis to answer his questions or calm his fears. I was really forced to trust God to take care of Jeff as well as to bring people into his life for support.

Jeff listened and continued to drive as I poured out as much as I could. When I came to the end of my confession, I wanted to know what he was thinking. There had been some confusion in Jeff's mind before I told him because he fully expected me to tell about someone else and not about myself. The awful thing he expected to hear was that his sister was pregnant! So when I started in on my eating disorder, he had to shift gears. But he adjusted, and so did I. He was glad Jenny was not pregnant, but here again was someone who connected sexual immorality to being the worst secret a person could admit.

When we arrived at school, I felt empty, alone, and unsure of myself. I didn't know what to expect as we got out of the car. I was drained! John pulled in behind us, and I just wanted things to look normal—whatever that was! Jeff's coming around from his side of the car to embrace me tipped John off that his prayers had been answered. I didn't know John had been praying for us, and he didn't know I was telling Jeff. He only knew to pray.

Jeff's embrace felt good that day! There was warmth, understanding, and strength in those arms that enfolded my vulnerability. He didn't fully comprehend all I had told him, and he had many questions on his mind, but Jeff knew enough. He was able to receive the truth, and me, knowing that we could go on.

That night after we left, Jeff was upset and needed someone to talk to, and God provided a friend. I had wanted to be the one there for him, but that simply wasn't possible. But God in His goodness knew better for us both.

God showed me that I didn't have to have all my bases covered with Jeff. It was not my responsibility to make sure he fully understood or that he would seek out the right people at the right time to talk with. God had those things under control. The groundwork with God had already been laid for Jeff, and it was Jeff's responsibility to tap into Him. I had done my part in finally telling my son the truth; God could certainly be trusted with the rest.

Throughout the year it has been interesting to talk with Jeff. He has questioned me more about the mechanics of an eating disorder than anyone so far. I'm glad he doesn't assume anything, but there have been times when he has brought to the surface some of the memories I thought I could keep buried. Jeff has wanted to know the specific: what I ate, how much, how often, where, and how could I ever do THAT? There has been a certain embarrassment on my part to answer him. Shame has wanted to rear its ugly head. Jeff asks these questions in the presence of John and Jenny. I have found them to be all ears! They too have wanted answers to questions they haven't dared ask. These questions always seem to come in the kitchen when I am preparing food. I do believe God has a sense of humor as we become honest before Him!

The Tuesday after Mother's Day I received Jeff's Mother's Day letter. It is one of those I tucked away to be reread when I begin to have doubts about my exposure and honesty with him. His closing paragraph simply read, "I love you a lot and pray for you daily! Keep writing your book! You have a lot to offer! I appreciate your openness to me about your past. I feel closer to you because of it." Those words are like a soothing balm embracing my soul. Never in a lifetime did I feel I would ever receive those words from Jeff.

Why? I had believed the lies the enemy of my being had fed me for years. Through my exposure I have seen that God is truly good, and can be trusted.

It has proven to be quite a year for me as I risked telling my "big" secret. I never thought I would tell anyone, much less be free to discuss it with them. It has been painful to admit my failures and expose my lies, but out of that pain I feel good for the first time in my life. Good to be known and loved, good to be free, and good to give something of myself that is really me.

Chapter Ten

After Recovery

In thinking through this final chapter, I've had mixed emotions on the "correct" way to end the journey I've taken you through my life. It is probably because I am embarking down a new and different path now that the chains of my secret have been broken. Many of my destructive patterns, both physical and mental, have changed, and as a result I am left with new situations to work my way through.

For Jenny—Permission Granted

Probably the toughest dynamics that have come into play since my recovery concern Jenny. When Jenny left home and entered her freshman year in college, she found herself on the campus of a Christian college living with girls practicing eating disorders similar to the ones I perpetuated. These girls were easy for Jenny to spot since I had openly shared with her about my life. She witnessed the classic symptoms of sneaking food from the cafeteria, binging, and the evidence of vomitus in wastebaskets and toilets. On one hand Jenny was not shocked by their behavior, yet on the other hand she was not prepared to deal with their anger, control, lies, and manipulation as she expressed her concern. Why? Because they reminded her of me!

At age nineteen, Jenny was mourning the fact that her mother had been unable to enter her pain as a young girl. She was overwhelmed with fear, frustration, and sadness as she saw the cycle being repeated in her dormitory. I am not surprised this happened to Jenny, but somehow I thought these feelings would not be provoked until she was older — possibly when she was married with a daughter of her own. Yet here I was sitting with Jenny as she sobbed, not over her friends with eating disorders, but over the loss she felt from what our relationship could have been if I had not lied and manipulated her.

I felt terrible and so much at fault for Jenny's pain. I could do nothing except enfold her in my arms and cry with her. I fought surges of panic, wondering just how much my eating disorder had damaged her. I wanted to fix the situation, but I couldn't.

At the time I didn't realize this was a turning point for Jenny. She drew strength and confidence from our tears because she was given permission to talk and tell me just how much she had been hurt. I never set out to hurt either of my children, but I know I have. Yet out of the discomfort, pain, and tears have come the freedom for Jenny and me to frankly face our struggles — together.

This incident illustrates one of the most important aspects of recovery: talking. Keeping secrets kills relationships and can kill you. Only through honest communication can relationships be restored. No matter how painful the secrets may be, giving someone the permission to talk about them could be the greatest gift you could ever give.

Jeff's Eye-opener

During Jeff's junior year in a Christian university (different from Jenny's), he found himself very much aware of girls on campus with obvious eating disorders. He knew what to look for after my exposure to him that previous summer, and he began to recognize the extreme thinness of one particular girl. One evening in his dorm room this girl became the topic of conversation among a group of Jeff's male friends. They agreed she was anorexic. They thought she looked great. They did not care she was starving herself to maintain the image. It did not matter that her dieting methods were unhealthy. They did not care what she had to do as long as she continued to look the way she did.

Jeff was the only one who did not agree with this assessment, and he told them so. He was troubled by their shallow thinking and wondered how many girls felt the pressure of thinness at any price, especially from their male counterparts. Jeff was especially alarmed as he thought of the possibilty of his sister being placed under the same pressure.

That evening reinforced for Jeff what he was coming to realize already: He was in the minority in his thinking. Jeff stood alone as he voiced his concern for this problem. His spirit is sensitive to girls and the pressures our society places on them to look a certain way. Jeff's eyes are not dimmed to view only the outward appearance, but are keen to see what lies beneath.

I don't know what it will take to sharpen the eyes and quicken the hearts of our society to see the dangerous magnitude of eating disorders. According to the National Association of Anorexia Nervosa and Associated Disorders, eating disorders are considered to be at an epidemic level. It is a crime that deaths from eating disorders, such as Karen Carpenter's, impact our society for only a short period before we forget and fall back into our old way of thinking.

In the appendix I have listed some of the warning signs for a person with an eating disorder, along with some of the dangerous physical side effects. Possibly these will serve as an eyeopener for you as you sharpen your awareness of eating disorders.

John—A Man of His Word

The day I told John about my secret, he promised not to tell anyone. He said, "This is your story to tell—it is safe with me." At the time I hadn't even thought to ask him not to tell, but as the months went by, I realize how very important his words were to me.

First, John kept his promise—he told no one. Even as the months marched by, he did not pressure me to speak to anyone, including our children. I felt no urgency from John; he was patient with me.

Second, even in the shame of my exposure, John held me in a position of respect. He did not demand information from me, and he did not negatively speculate the impact of this information on others. He respected me enough to know I would tell others when the timing was right.

Third, John has never thrown those twenty-five years back in my face to shame me. In other words, he has played fair. He has been angry over what I've done—I know this because he has told me so—but he has not used his anger against me to get his way, to prove his point, or to provoke pity. He would have been justified in doing so, but he knows the irreparable damage it could do to our relationship. Thank God that John knew this without ever putting me in a position to defend myself against him. A situation like that could only breed disaster!

Fourth, John has not only listened to me, he has heard me. This has been vitally important as I've poured out the secrets of my past. Along with this he's given the gift of time. He placed no time frame on me to work through this process. He has simply allowed me to move at my own pace. At times I forged ahead; at other times I seemed to be standing still or slipping back into my sinful relational patterns. John has been patient to stand by me no matter where I've been in the process.

Obviously, John has done many things well. He has been my companion as I've come out of hiding and disorder. We've worked together. I can't stress enough how important it is to come alongside people with secrets and disorder, and to patiently and lovingly stay with them through their exposure. John has certainly modeled this support for me.

What Choices Will You Make?

Life is full of choices. My story is full of the choices I've made—some good and some bad. Yet to fully recover from my eating disorder, I chose God. Healing is found at the foot of the Cross, no matter when we come or how broken our spirit is on arrival. I continually find myself at this place as the process of recovery is being worked out in my life. Recovery is a process. When I want to blame others, feel sorry for myself, stiffen my neck in self-justification, or simply wonder, "What's the use?" I know I need God.

God does work in the recovery process regardless of the paths we take. I did not take a clinical or therapeutic path. My arrogance kept me hiding, and my stubbornness said, "I'll die first!" I wish I could say I am the only eating-disordered person who has felt this way, but I am not. Unfortunately, I have talked with others who have a similar mindset. It is a dangerous way to think and live.

Help is available if you choose to seek it out. My story gives the route I took and my struggles along the way. I have known women who chose hospitalization, medication, or counseling as their route to recovery. These methods do work; in fact, they are necessary for people with life-threatening eating disorders. I've also talked with others who, like myself, did not choose any of these methods and have recovered. How? I don't believe there is any one answer, except to say, that the grace of God knows no limits. His ways are a mystery that cause us to marvel.

Yet, there is one thing I do know: Whichever method you choose, remember that only God can truly comfort, bring gladness out of sadness, a spirit of praise out of a spirit of fainting, and ultimately restore ashes to beauty in the broken-hearted (Isaiah 61:3).

Warning Signs and Side Effects of Eating Disorders

The following information is from the National Association of Anorexia Nervosa and Associated Disorders (ANAD), founded in 1976. ANAD provides a multi-faceted program for people with eating disorders, and all services are free of charge. ANAD has been most helpful in providing this information, and through this contact I discovered a group of people who are truly committed to assisting those with eating disorders and their families.

ANAD
Box 7
Highland Park, Illinois 60035
(708) 831-3438

Warning Signs of Anorexia Nervosa
*Deliberate self-starvation with weight loss
*Intense, persistent fear of gaining weight
*Refusal to eat, except for tiny portions
*Continuous dieting
*Compulsive exercise
*Excessive facial/body hair
*Distorted body image
*Abnormal weight loss
*Sensitivity to cold
*Absent or irregular menstruation
*Hair loss

Warning Signs of Bulimia Nervosa
*Preoccupation with food
*Binge eating, usually in secret
*Vomiting after binging
*Abuse of laxatives, diuretics, diet pills, or emetics
*Compulsive exercising
*Swollen salivary glands
*Broken blood vessels in eyes

Psychological Repercussions from Both Disorders
*Depression
*Shame and guilt
*Mood swings
*Low self-esteem
*Withdrawal
*Impaired family and social relationships
*"All or nothing" thinking
*Perfectionism

Partial Listing of Physical Problems Brought about by Eating Disorders

	External Problems	Internal Problems	Causes
Skin	Dryness Fine Rash Pimples	Dehydration	Reduced fluid intake. Excessive fluid elimination. Frequent vomiting. Laxative abuse.
Salivary glands	Swelling, pain, tenderness	Possible infection — not usually	Frequent vomiting.
Constipation		Insufficient material Insufficient fluid. Dulled intestinal nerves.	Failure to take in or retain sufficient food and fluid. Laxative abuse.
Edema (water retention)	Swelling and puffiness, more frequently ankles and feet.	Electrolyte imbalance. Perhaps general systems problems	Malnutrition. Frequent vomiting. Excessive laxatives or diuretics.

	External Problems	*Internal Problems*	*Causes*
Bloating	Swelling over stomach or abdominal area.	Electrolyte imbalance. Time required for body systems to adjust. Insufficient protein intake.	Long periods of starvation and probable excessive vomiting, laxatives, or diuretics.
Abdominal pain		Peptides. Hunger pangs. Change in the bowels.	Failure to identify hunger. Emotional attitudes. Insufficient intake.
Feeling of fullness.	Slight distention after eating is normal.	Normal feeling after eating for everybody.	Fear. Emotional attitudes.
Teeth	Frequent cavities. Frequent cavities plus erosion of enamel.		Inadequate diet. Frequent vomiting or regurgitation. Diet limited to citrus fruits or abnormal carbohydrate intake.
Amenorrhea	No menstrual period.	Inability to produce hormones.	Lack of body fat, rigorous athletic training, emotional attitudes, sometimes gorging/ purging.

If you are aware of people struggling with eating disorders, it is my hope you will pursue them, stay in relationship with them, and be ready to love them well through whichever path of recovery is necessary. Don't be quick to judge, to solve their problems, or to expose their secrets.

Sooner or later in the recovery process, any person with an eating disorder must make some tough choices. One of the toughest simply could be to choose to live. Unfortunately, that is a choice no one can make for another.

Eating disorders are complex. Only God could unravel the complicated knots this disorder wove through my life. I trust my story has been an encouragement, possibly even an inspiration to begin the process of recovery for yourself. It is a journey, but one that can be taken. Just don't travel alone—I didn't. Many people were my companions along the way, some staying longer than others. Yet only God went the entire distance with me from start to finish. He is my constant companion as I continue to move through the process He began in my life. He wants to be yours, as well!

Types of Sexual Abuse: Contact and Interaction

CONTACT

Very Severe: Genital intercourse (forcible or nonforcible); oral or anal sex (forcible or nonforcible)

Severe: Unclothed genital contact, including manual touching or penetration (forcible or nonforcible); unclothed breast contact (forcible or nonforcible); simulated intercourse

Least Severe: Sexual kissing (forcible or nonforcible); sexual touching of buttocks, thighs, legs, or clothed breasts or genitals

INTERACTIONS

Verbal: Direct solicitation for sexual purposes; seductive (subtle) solicitation or innuendo; description of sexual practices; repeated use of sexual language and sexual terms as personal names

Visual: Exposure to or use for pornography; intentional (repeated) exposure to sexual acts, sexual organs, and/or sexually provocative attire (bra, nighties, slip, underwear); inappropriate attention (scrutiny) directed toward body (clothed or unclothed) or clothing for purpose of sexual stimulation

Psychological: Physical/sexual boundary violation: Intrusive interest in menstruation, clothing, pubic development; repeated use of enemas

Sexual/relational boundary violation: Intrusive interest in child's sexual activity, use of child as a spouse surrogate (confidant, intimate companion, protector, or counselor)